AQA

Psychology for GCSE

THIRD EDITION

Understanding Psychology

bara Woods

l Holt, Rob Lewis and Victoria Carrington

HODDER
EDUCATION
AN HACHETTE UK COMPANY

Orders: please contact Bookpoint Ltd, 130 Milton Park, Abingdon, Oxon OX14 4SB.
Telephone: (44) 01235 827720. Fax: (44) 01235 400454. Lines are open from 9.00–
5.00, Monday to Saturday, with a 24-hour message answering service. You can also
order through our website www.hoddereducation.co.uk

If you have any comments to make about this, or any of our other titles, please
send them to
educationenquiries@hodder.co.uk

British Library Cataloguing in Publication Data
A catalogue record for this title is available from the British Library

ISBN: 978 0 340 98531 1

First Edition Published 2002
Second Edition Published 2004
This Edition Published 2009

Impression number   10 9 8 7 6 5 4 3 2 1
Year   2012 2011 2010 2009

Copyright © 2009 Barbara Woods, Vicky Carrington, Nigel Holt and Rob Lewis

Hachette UK's policy is to use papers that are natural, renewable and recyclable
products and made from wood grown in sustainable forests. The logging and
manufacturing processes are expected to conform to the environmental
regulations of the country of origin.

Cover photo © Imagezoo/Imagescom
Illustrations by Barking Dog Art
Typeset by Fakenham Photosetting Limited, Fakenham, Norfolk
Printed in Italy

CONTENTS

INTRODUCTION

This textbook provides an introduction to the work and ideas of psychologists, covering topics such as memory, learning, sex and gender, and prejudice. This edition has been written to accompany the recently amended AQA specification for GCSE Psychology, and is relevant to students studying both the full and short GCSE course.

Each chapter covers a topic on the specification and has sample exam questions throughout. Research and theories are evaluated and examples of their application to everyday life are discussed.

Throughout the book there are 'boxes' of text that provide suggestions for student activities. These enable students to work with the material and so increase their understanding of it. Key terms are given in highlighted boxes in order to stress their importance, and a glossary at the back provides explanations for frequently used terms.

The AQA provides a GCSE Psychology specification, teachers' guide and specimen papers and mark schemes, all of which provide essential information for teachers of the specification. For further reading, many of the textbooks written for Advanced-level students provide suitable material, and the AQA publishes a list of books in their teachers' guide. A teacher's resource pack will accompany this edition.

Our aim has been to update and amend the original book to ensure it is suitable for a wide range of abilities, and to also include sufficient information to enable students to achieve an A grade. We hope that you find it enjoyable and stimulating, and that it enables you to enjoy this fascinating subject and perhaps take it further.

Victoria Carrington
Nigel Holt
Rob Lewis
Barbara Woods

2009

ACKNOWLEDGEMENTS

I would like to dedicate this book to the memory of my dear mum Susan Carrington: for all of your time, friendship and, most of all, your encouragement and inspiration. I couldn't have got this far without you.

Thanks to my dad for all of his support, to Dave for his patience and endless cups of tea, and, as promised, to my Helen, Jane and Danielle … there you go, you are now famous.

My thanks go to Ruben Hale at Hodder Education for allowing me the opportunity to do this. His enthusiasm and patience have been remarkable.

The author and publishers would like to thank the following for permission to use photographs:

p. 13 NPG x71365 Sir Frederic Charles Bartlett by Bassano, half-plate film negative, 5 February 1948 © National Portrait Gallery, London; p. 31 © Paul Ekman Ph.D; p. 43 © Chris Ware/Keystone/Getty Images; p. 56 © 2005 Roger-Viollet / Topfoto; p. 59 © Paramount Pictures / Album / AKG; p. 62 © Bob Adelman/Corbis; p. 63 © Hayley Madden/Redferns/Getty Images; p. 77 © Mario Tama/Getty Images; p. 80 © 2009 Oxford Scientific/Photolibrary.com; p. 92 © Mansell/Time Life Pictures/Getty Images; p. 100 © Oxford Scientific Films/Photolibrary.com; p. 112 © Imagno/Thomas Sessler Verlag/Getty Images; p. 120 © 1965 by Stanley Milgram from the film *Obedience*, with kind permission by Alexandra Milgram; p. 126 With kind permission of Philip Zimbardo, Inc.; p. 143 © Bettmann/Corbis; p. 149 © William Britten / iStockphoto.com; p. 152 © KEYTE, GILES / TIGER ASPECT PICS / THE KOBAL COLLECTION; p. 160 © Konstantin Sutyagin – fotolia.com; p. 165 With kind permission by Alfred Bandura; p. 166 With kind permission by Alfred Bandura.

While every effort has been made to trace copyright holders, this has not been possible in all cases; any omissions brought to our attention will be remedied in future printings.

MAKING SENSE OF OTHER PEOPLE

CHAPTER 1

Memory

ASK YOURSELF

How good is your memory?

- How often do you use it?
- Write down how you have used your memory in the last 30 minutes.
- What would life be like if you lost your memory?

PROCESSES OF ENCODING, STORAGE AND RETRIEVAL

Life would be very difficult if we didn't have a memory. You wouldn't be able to get to school or college, recognise yourself in the mirror, or get yourself dressed in the morning. In a way, we take our memory for granted, don't we? When you are sitting in a lesson you have to process the information that you are receiving, whether it is reading a chapter in a book or listening to your teacher. Whatever you read enters your eyes as light, and what you hear enters your ears as sound. What happens once you have received this information? It goes through three processes: encoding, storage and

KEY TERM

Encoding – information is changed or encoded so that it can be stored. This can be done visually (through images), acoustically (through sound) or semantically (by meaning).

ASK YOURSELF

If you have ever been asked to remember something, for example a shopping list, how do you remember it? Do you visualise the list that you left at home or the items that you need (for example fruit in the fruit bowl), do you say it over and over again (acoustic), or do you attach some sort of meaning to it, for example telling a story with the items?

retrieval. This raw information is processed by your visual and hearing systems and then sent to your brain.

We all have our own ways of remembering or **encoding** information – that is why we are all different when it comes to memory.

The information received is then **stored**. This happens so that we can access it at a later date. We store different types of information in different ways and this affects how we **retrieve** it at a later date. Failure to retrieve it means that we can't remember it.

When we look at the differences between short-term memory and long-term memory and their features, we need to consider them in terms of **duration** and **capacity**.

KEY TERMS

Storage – encoded information is stored in the memory so that it can be accessed at a later date.

Retrieval – accessing or retrieving the information from storage.

Duration – how long information can stay with that memory (this can be anything from a few seconds or minutes up to a lifetime).

Capacity – how much information can be stored with that memory (this can be anything from a few items up to the capacity being limitless).

EXPLANATIONS OF MEMORY

The multi-store model of memory

One explanation that was put forward in 1968 was the **multi-store model** of memory. Richard Atkinson and Richard Shiffrin suggested that memory has separate stores (sensory memory, short term and long term).

They proposed that memory is a process that goes through a series of stores

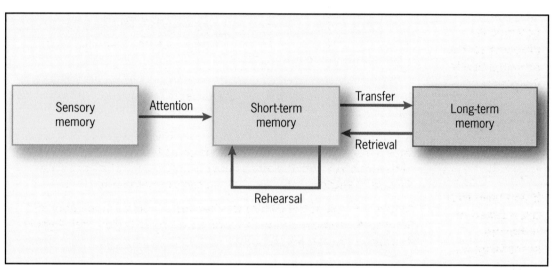

Figure 1.1 The multi-store model of memory

Sensory memory is the start of the process. We pay attention to some of the information that we receive through our senses. This is held very briefly, for just a few seconds (the duration), in the sensory memory store. The information is stored in its original form (speech is stored as sounds, visual is stored as images). The information is then passed on to the short-term memory for encoding.

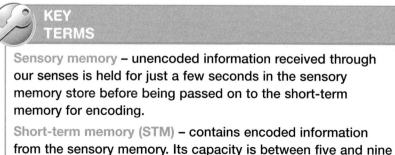

KEY TERMS

Sensory memory – unencoded information received through our senses is held for just a few seconds in the sensory memory store before being passed on to the short-term memory for encoding.

Short-term memory (STM) – contains encoded information from the sensory memory. Its capacity is between five and nine objects, and its duration is up to 30 seconds.

Short-term memory contains any information that has been encoded from the sensory memory. George Miller (1956) claimed that we can hold anything between five and nine objects in our short-term memory (known as the magic number: 7 +/– 2).

Once we have this capacity, any new information that comes along pushes out (displaces) the old information that is already there. Information in the short-term memory is usually encoded acoustically (as we hear it) or visually (as we see it) and has duration of up to 30 seconds. If it is rehearsed, it can transfer into the long-term memory.

EXAM STYLE QUESTION

Complete the following table for short-term memory.

Capacity	Duration	Encoding

ACTIVITY

Test your memory
This activity is known as a digit span and it is to test your short-term memory. In pairs, take it in turns to read out the following list of numbers. Do one line at a time and get your partner to read it back to you:

387
1278
34556
987321
5342214
98434568
887231732

How did you do? You should have found that the more numbers there were, the more difficult it became to remember them all.

When you were remembering the numbers in this activity, were you grouping the numbers together, for example 887 231 732?

Figure 1.2 How do you remember telephone numbers?

If so, this is a process called **chunking** and it is a way to improve the capacity of the short-term memory.

We all probably do this if we are asked to remember something like a telephone number.

ACTIVITY

Have a go at chunking these numbers:

01712341123
08702387732

KEY STUDY

Bower and Springston (1970)

Aim: To test the effects of chunking.

Method: They had two groups of participants. The control group was presented with groups of letters such as: FB, IPH, DTW, AIB and M. The experimental group was given the same letters but grouped differently: FBI, PHD, CIA and IBM. You can see that, when arranged like this, the letters 'make sense' to us, so we automatically 'chunk' them.

Results: The experimental group recalled many more letters than the control group.

Conclusion: The researchers concluded that 'chunking' increases the capacity of short-term memory. These groups of three letters refer to things we already know. FBI is the Federal Bureau of Investigation, for instance. This information is stored elsewhere in our memory: the long-term store.

RESEARCH METHODS

The G. Bower and F. Springston study is an example of a laboratory experiment. An explanation of a laboratory experiment and its advantages and disadvantages can be found in Chapter 5: Research methods and ethics – part 1, pages 70–71.

So, to do chunking we need to use our long-term memory.

The difference between short-term memory and long-term memory is illustrated in free-recall experiments. A free-recall experiment is when participants are asked to remember a list of items in no particular order.

KEY STUDY

Murdock (1962)

Aim: Bennet Murdock wanted to investigate free recall and its effect on a person's memory.

Method: He gave participants a number of words to remember and then asked them to recall as many as possible, in any order.

Results: The first words to be recalled were those the participants heard last (the recency effect); this is evidence that the last few words were still stored in short-term memory.

The other words recalled were those heard first (the primacy effect).

Conclusion: When we are asked to recall a list of words, we remember the first words on the list well and the last words on the list well. Murdock (1962) says that this is because the first words on the list have been encoded, have made it into the long-term memory and are recalled from there. The last words on the list do not have time to be encoded, and so are recalled straight from the short-term memory.

RESEARCH METHODS

The Murdock study is an example of a laboratory experiment. An explanation of a laboratory experiment and its advantages and disadvantages can be found in Chapter 5: Research methods and ethics – part 1, pages 70–71.

Long-term memory

The long-term memory can be seen as the 'storehouse' of all things in memory that are not currently being used but can be retrieved (got hold of) at any time.

The **duration** of information that reaches the long-term memory can be anything from a few minutes up to a lifetime.

The **capacity** of the long-term memory is unlimited – basically our long-term memory is never full, although it can sometimes feel like that when trying to revise!

Encoding in the long-term memory can be visual or acoustic (like the short-term memory), or semantic, which means to give it some sort of meaning.

EXAM STYLE QUESTIONS

Complete the following table for the long-term memory.

Capacity	Duration	Encoding

State three differences between the short-term memory and the long-term memory.

Evidence to support the multi-store model of memory comes from cases where people have lost their short-term memory (due to an accident) but kept their long-term memory, or sometimes the other way round.

ASK YOURSELF

What does this suggest about the multi-store model and how does it support it?

⚖ **EVALUATION BOX**

- The multi-store model provides a simple description of memory processes.
- Atkinson and Shiffrin used a scientific approach to carry out their research.
- There is research to support the idea of separate memory stores.
- It has been criticised for its focus on memory for new facts, such as word lists and numbers. This is why the model seems to explain how we remember a telephone number until we dial it, but cannot explain many of our everyday experiences of memory.

✏ **EXAM STYLE QUESTIONS**

1 Using your knowledge of psychology, outline the multi-store model of memory.
2 Evaluate the multi-store model of memory in terms of strengths and weaknesses.

Levels of processing

Another model of memory was put forward by Fergus Craik and Robert Lockhart in 1972. It's called the levels of processing theory. They agreed with Atkinson and Shiffrin that short-term memory and long-term memory were separate stores, but they interpreted it in a different way. They suggested that whether or not we remember information depends on what we do with the information when it comes in. They proposed that we process information at two different levels: deep and shallow.

For example, if you had to remember a telephone number and you were using acoustic encoding (saying it over and over again), this doesn't involve you thinking about it very deeply. So we process it at a shallow level and, as a result, this can be easily and quickly forgotten. In contrast, if you tried to remember the number by linking it to other familiar numbers, for example your date of birth or house number, you are processing it at a deeper level.

A study that was conducted to test this theory was done by Craik and Endel Tulving.

KEY STUDY

Craik and Tulving (1975)

Aim: To see if the level at which information is processed has an effect on a person's memory.

Method: They told participants that their study was to test speed of reaction and perception. They presented them with a word, very quickly, then a question about the word. There were three different ways of testing the levels of processing concept:

1 The structural level of the word: e.g. 'Is the word in upper-case letters?'
2 The phonetic level: e.g. 'Does the word rhyme with …?'
3 The semantic level: e.g. 'Does the word go in this sentence?'

Participants were then given a long list of words and asked which ones they had seen earlier during the experiment.

Results:

Level of processing required	Question asked	Words recognised later
Structural level (appearance)	Is the word in upper-case letters?	18%
Phonetic level (sound)	Does the word rhyme with …?	50%
Semantic level (meaning)	Does the word go in this sentence?	80%

Conclusion: This shows that more words were recalled if participants had to think about their meaning than if they had to look at their appearance. Therefore, the more deeply the material had to be processed, the more likely they were to remember it.

RESEARCH METHODS

The Craik and Tulving study is an example of a laboratory experiment. An explanation of a laboratory experiment and its advantages and disadvantages can be found Chapter 5: Research methods and ethics – part 1, pages 70–71.

ACTIVITY

Draw a bar chart to display the findings of this study: be sure to give it an appropriate title and label your axis correctly.

ACTIVITY

Have a go at devising your own experiment on levels of processing. First of all you need a list of words, then use the questions that Craik and Tulving used to go with them. Once you have done that, answer the following questions:

1 Identify your sampling method.
2 State one advantage and one disadvantage of your sampling method.
3 Devise a hypothesis.
4 Identify your independent and dependent variables.
5 What type of method are you using?
6 State one advantage and one disadvantage of the method.
7 Identify the experimental design.
8 State one advantage and one disadvantage of the experimental design.

EVALUATION BOX

- There is a great deal of support for the levels of processing theory.
- The majority of research that has been conducted has been laboratory based, so the behaviour can be classed as being artificial.
- Atkinson and Shiffrin used a scientific approach to carry out their research.
- It doesn't explain why deeper processing helps memory.
- Deeper processing takes more time than shallow processing, so this might be the reason for remembering more information.

The reconstructive approach

The final approach that we will consider as an explanation of memory is the reconstructive approach, which was developed by Frederic Bartlett in 1932. Although it is a very old theory, it has received a huge amount of support.

Figure 1.3 Frederic Bartlett

Bartlett said that memory was an active process. He said that we use existing knowledge, which he called **schemas**, to understand new information and impose some sort of meaning on it. He demonstrated this in his famous 'war of the ghosts' research. *The war of the ghosts* is a North American folk story, which is shown below:

The war of the ghosts

One night two young men from Egulac went down to the river to hunt seals and while they were there it became foggy and calm. Then they heard war-cries, and they thought: 'Maybe this is a war-party.' They escaped to the shore, and hid behind a log. Now canoes came up, and they heard the noise of paddles, and saw one canoe coming up to them. There were five men in the canoe, and they said:

'What do you think? We wish to take you along. We are going up the river to make war on the people.'

One of the young men said: 'I have no arrows.'

'Arrows are in the canoe,' they said.

'I will not go along. I might be killed. My relatives do not know where I have gone. But you,' he said, turning to the other, 'may go with them.'

So one of the young men went, but the other returned home.

And the warriors went on up the river to a town on the other side of Kalama. The people came down to the water, and they began to fight, and many were killed. But presently the young man heard one of the warriors say: 'Quick, let us go home: that Indian has been hit.' Now he thought: 'Oh, they are ghosts.' He did not feel sick, but they said he had been shot.

So the canoes went back to Egulac, and the young man went ashore to his house and made a fire. And he told everybody and said: 'Behold, I accompanied the ghosts, and we went to fight. Many of our fellows were killed, and many of those who attacked us were killed. They said I was hit, and I did not feel sick.'

He told it all, and then he became quiet. When the sun rose he fell down. Something black came out of his mouth. His face became contorted. The people jumped up and cried.

He was dead.

KEY STUDY

Bartlett (1932)

Aim: To test the idea that people use existing knowledge to understand new information.

Method: Participants were given *The war of the ghosts* to read. Once they had read it, they were asked to recall everything that they could about the story (over varying periods from a few hours to several months).

Results: Bartlett found that the majority of people added their own meaning to the story and reconstructed their memories to try to make sense of the information. In particular, he noticed that they:

- Missed out some details and added new details
- Added emphasis to some parts
- Changed the order of the incidents.

Conclusion: Bartlett said that we use schemas to help us fill in gaps in our memories of things.

An example of a schema that we all have is a 'kitchen schema'. This has been tested by showing participants photographs of various places and either adding something unusual (such as a football) that you wouldn't expect to be found there, or missing something deliberate out (such as a cooker). As Bartlett suggested, people fill the gaps by using their schemas.

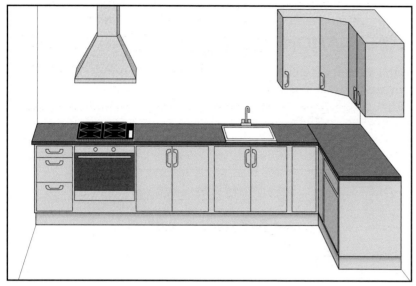

Figure 1.4 A kitchen schema

ACTIVITY

Have a go at reading *The war of the ghosts* to your friends at the start of the day. Ask them to recall it immediately. Then ask them to recall it at the end of the day. See if your results support Bartlett's theory.

EVALUATION BOX

- The theory was put forward before the other two theories that we have looked at and is now very dated. The multi-store and levels of processing models have used more scientific approaches to test their theories.
- The 'war of the ghosts' study can be criticised as it is quite artificial (not similar to everyday experiences). When researchers have asked participants to recollect their own real-life experiences they have found that, each time they were asked, their recollections were very similar.

EXPLANATIONS OF FORGETTING

In this section we will consider a number of different explanations for why we forget things. It is important to look at reasons why we forget, just like it is to look at reasons why we remember information. Psychologists are interested in the processes involved in forgetting.

ASK YOURSELF

Do you think that we do forget information, or is it merely because we can't access it?

Figure 1.5 Why do we forget things?

Interference theory

The theory itself suggests that our memory may be affected in a negative way by information that we have already stored, or by new experiences that occur while we are taking in the information.

Retroactive interference occurs when new information interferes with the ability to recall old information. For example, if somebody can speak French and then starts learning German, if they try to speak French they may only remember the German words. This is because they have a good, well-used memory for the French words, and the new German words interfere with that memory.

Proactive interference is the opposite. Proactive interference occurs when old information (something that you already know) interferes with your ability to take in new information. For example, you go to do your weekly shop at the supermarket and the store has been moved about; you still go to the old place for your coffee.

KEY STUDY

Underwood and Postman (1960)

Aim: To test the retroactive theory in an experimental set-up.

Method: The researchers asked participants to learn a list of paired words, for example: cat–tree, book–tractor. Half of the participants then learned a second list, for example: cat–glass, book–revolver. As you can see, in the second list the first word of the pair is the same as the first word in the original list, but the second word is different. A second group (a control group) was not given the second list. Participants in both groups were then asked to recall the words in the first list.

Results: The researchers found that recall in the control group, who only learned the first list, was more accurate than in the other group.

Conclusion: This suggests that learning the items in the second list interfered with the participants' ability to recall the first list.

RESEARCH METHODS

The Underwood and Postman study is an example of a laboratory experiment. An explanation of a laboratory experiment and its advantages and disadvantages can be found in Chapter 5: Research methods and ethics – part 1, pages 70–71.

EVALUATION BOX

- The majority of research that has been conducted has been based on laboratory experiments, often using artificial tasks. Therefore, the results cannot be generalised to other people, places and settings.
- The theory may explain why people find it difficult to learn two similar languages.

Amnesia

An alternative explanation for why people forget is amnesia. There are two types: retrograde and anterograde amnesia. **Retrograde**

amnesia is a form of amnesia where someone will be unable to recall events that occurred before the development of amnesia. **Anterograde amnesia** is a loss of memory of what happens after the event that caused the amnesia.

In most cases of anterograde amnesia, patients lose the ability to recall facts. For instance, they are able to remember and, in some cases, learn how to do things such as talk on the phone or ride a bicycle, but they may not remember what they have eaten for lunch earlier that day.

In retrograde amnesia the memory loss may affect specific classes of memory. For example, a concert pianist with retrograde amnesia may still remember what a piano is but may forget how to play.

A case study by Robert Ornstein, Richard Thompson and David Macaulay (1984), which demonstrates anterograde amnesia, is that of H. M. (these are the person's initials – this is to protect confidentiality). H. M. had been suffering epileptic fits since he was 16 years old. At the age of 27 he underwent a radical surgical procedure to try to cure his epilepsy. His epilepsy was cured; however, because the hippocampus (part of the brain) was removed on both sides of his brain, he was left with anterograde amnesia. His memory of events prior to the surgery was near normal but he could not remember anything after the surgical procedure. For example, within the first few hours after his operation, he was unable to find his bedroom in the hospital and could not recognise the doctors and nurses. H. M.'s short-term memory was normal: he could retain information for about 15 seconds without rehearsal and for longer when he used rehearsal. However, he could not transfer information into his long-term memory.

EYEWITNESS TESTIMONY

Faces are extremely important things to humans. When we are young it is important to be able to recognise the most important faces in our lives: usually our parents'. When we are older, it is important to be able to recognise the faces of people we know and people we trust, people who we want to (or should!) avoid, and faces of people we need to find in a crowd for some reason.

In terms of eyewitness testimony, memory for faces is extremely important. Identifying the face of someone who has committed a crime can mean the difference between their being arrested and prosecuted, or their getting away with it entirely.

ACTIVITY

Imagine you were an eyewitness to a crime – what factors do you think would affect your recall of the event?

How do we recognise faces?

V. Bruce and A. Young (1986) developed a model that suggests how facial perception, and our memory for faces, work. They suggested that there are three separate stages in the process of looking at a face and remembering it (Bruce and Young, 1998):

1 In the first stage, we don't see the whole face at all. Instead we see a set of individual features: we examine the eyes, mouth, hairline, nose and everything else that makes up a face, separately. By looking at a person's mouth and their eyes we can tell whether someone is happy or sad; we can also tell how old a person is from their facial features.

2 In the next stage we put all the parts together to form a whole face. This provides us with a 'mental picture' of the face we are looking at.

3 We use this mental picture for the third stage of the process, where we 'look up' the face in our memory. This lets us know whether the person is someone we know, or someone we may have seen before.

One of the most important parts of this model is the cognitive system: this is where we store all sorts of useful information about faces. For instance, we know that when someone cries it usually means that they are sad, and when someone laughs it is usually because they are happy. We also know that we are very unlikely to see Prince Charles in our local supermarket! This means that if we see a face with features that look like those of Prince Charles, or any other famous person, when shopping, we know that it's very unlikely to actually be this person. This knowledge helps us to correctly identify the faces we see.

Reliability of eyewitness testimony

Research conducted into eyewitness testimony has highlighted the fact that it is not too reliable and, as a result of this, it has led to a number of changes nowadays as to how the police and the courts use the information given by eyewitnesses.

Facial recognition and eyewitness testimony

The 'cognitive' part of Bruce and Young's model is very important when we think about eyewitness testimony. One way that we try to remember things is to imagine ourselves in the place in which we saw or experienced the thing we are trying to remember. If we were trying to remember a face, perhaps of someone we saw carrying out a crime, we might imagine ourselves in the place where we saw the crime happen. This helps the cognitive part of the face perception model to identify whether the face we are looking at, perhaps in a picture, is the same as the one we saw when we witnessed the crime.

Bruce and Young (1996) warned that facial processing is not just about recognising the features of a face, however. There is much more to it than that! They say that a face is much more than just a collection of features: a face carries all sorts of information about emotion and age, and our correct perception of these things can be influenced by our own experiences and our own abilities to read this information.

This is important when we think about how faces are identified by eyewitnesses. Very often a 'photofit' is used to help a witness describe a face: a kit is used to create a face from a collection of different eyes, mouths, chins, noses and hairlines. Bruce and Young (1996) say that it is not just the individual features that help us to identify a face; it is how those features work together that really provides us with our perception and, therefore, memory of a face. This is why correctly identifying a face with a photofit is so terribly difficult.

Memory recall and leading questions

Elizabeth Loftus investigated eyewitness testimony: she was interested in seeing whether people's memory for something they had witnessed might be altered when they tried to recall it later on. One of her most famous experiments highlighted the fact that questions can lead people to distort their accounts massively. These types of questions are called 'leading' questions. An example of a leading question is below. Read the scenario first.

Imagine you are in an assembly. The head teacher is talking about a number of thefts that have occurred from students' lockers. He is urging people to let him know if they have any information about it. You recall seeing a suspicious-looking person when you were in school late the other evening. You tell the head teacher after assembly. He asks you a number of questions, including: 'What colour were his trainers?'

'What colour were his trainers?' is a leading question. This may lead you to presume that he (if it was a male) had trainers on. Therefore, this may distort your account.

🧩 KEY STUDY

Loftus and Palmer (1974)

Aim: To test the effect of leading questions on a person's recall of an event.

Method: Elizabeth Loftus and John Palmer's study involved splitting participants into three groups (one of these was a control group). They all watched a film of a traffic accident. After watching the film they were asked a number of questions about the film, all the same except for a question about the speed of

KEY STUDY – (continued)

the cars when the accident happened. The independent variable in this case was the verb that was used in the question. The verbs were as follows:

- hit
- smashed.

The question was: 'How fast were the cars going when they *hit/smashed* the other car?' The control group were not asked this question.

Results:

	Hit	Smashed
Mean estimated speed	34mph	41mph

The results showed that those participants who had the verb 'smashed' reported seeing the car as going faster.

One week later, all of the participants answered some more questions. One of the key questions this time was whether they had seen any broken glass (there wasn't any in the film). Loftus and Palmer wanted to find out whether the different verbs they had used would influence the participants' memory of the event. The results were as follows:

Smashed	Hit	Control group
32%	14%	12%

Conclusion: Those participants who were asked about the cars smashing were more likely to report having seen the broken glass.

KEY STUDY – (continued)

People's memory of an event can be influenced by the questions that they are asked about it. These questions can therefore distort their long-term memory of the event.

What about the results of the control group? They weren't affected by the verbs as they hadn't been asked the question about the speed of the car, so why did 12 per cent of them report seeing the glass? The fact that they had been asked the question led them to believe that there had been glass there. This is known as a leading question.

RESEARCH METHODS

The Loftus and Palmer study is an example of a laboratory experiment. An explanation of a laboratory experiment and its advantages and disadvantages can be found in Chapter 5: Research methods and ethics – part 1, pages 70–71.

ACTIVITY

Draw a bar chart to display the two sets of findings above, making sure that you give it a title and label the axis.

ASK YOURSELF

How could this distort a witness's account in court?

The practical implications of this suggest that lawyers should not ask leading questions of witnesses. This also applies to police questioning.

EXAM STYLE QUESTIONS

Describe one study in which eyewitness testimony was investigated. Include in your answer the aim, method, results and conclusion.

PRACTICAL APPLICATIONS DERIVED FROM THE EXPLANATIONS OF MEMORY AND LEARNING

Improving memory

Several ideas for improving memory have been generated from the three explanations we have reviewed. Despite criticism that some of the research evidence used memories of nonsense syllables or unrelated words, there are some principles that we can apply to our everyday experiences that can help us remember more effectively. These include:

- Chunking facts to increase the capacity of short-term memory, for example saying a long telephone number in pairs of numbers rather than single digits
- Rehearsing information to increase retention in short-term memory, for example repeating someone's address until you can write it down
- Encoding information to aid transfer and storage (we look at several ways of doing this below)
- Working with information to increase the depth of processing and so improve retention, for example writing up notes from psychology class in your own words rather than simply reading this book, or making a hierarchy of topics, as described below under Organisation.

Encoding information to improve retention

Encoding simply means changing information so that it can be stored. We have already noted that, in the long term, information is usually stored by meaning and it is given meaning by its links to other information already stored in memory. Look at Bower and Springston's research on chunking (see Key Study on page 7). It is only because the trigrams (three letters) FBI or IBM have meaning for us that chunking works. This meaning is generated from the information we already have in our long-term memory.

Three of the ways in which we encode information are by organisation, by context and by elaboration. These processes also enable us to recall (or retrieve) the information we have stored, as you will see in the discussion of these processes that follows.

Organisation

W. A. Bousfield (1963) investigated whether we organise information in long-term memory.

KEY STUDY

Bousfield (1963)

Aim: To see if people organise information in long-term memory.

Method: He showed participants 60 randomly presented words and then asked them to recall the words in any order they wanted, using free recall. Words came from these four categories: vegetables, animals, professions and names.

Results: Results showed that the order in which the participants recalled the words was in clusters from the same category, such as mouse, cat, horse and donkey.

Conclusion: He concluded that people spontaneously organise information by meaning.

RESEARCH METHODS

The Bousfield study is an example of a laboratory experiment. An explanation of a laboratory experiment and its advantages and disadvantages can be found in Chapter 5: Research methods and ethics – part 1, pages 70–71.

Material can be also organised in a sequence (such as alphabetically or by size or time) to aid recall. Imagine a patient discharged from hospital whose treatment involved taking various pills at different times, changing a dressing and doing exercises. If the doctor gives these instructions in the order in which they must be carried out through the day, this will help the patient remember them.

Context

Retrieval of information can be improved when it is linked to the context in which it was learned. This is why you can remember what you went upstairs for if you go back to the room where you first thought about it.

🧩 KEY STUDY

Godden and Baddeley (1975)

Aim: To see if context improved a person's memory.

Method: D. Godden and A. Baddeley asked deep-sea divers to memorise a list of words. One group did this on a beach and the other group were five metres under water. When they were asked to remember the words, the groups were divided. Half of the beach learners remained on the beach but the rest had to recall underwater. Half of the underwater learners remained there, but the other half had to recall on the beach.

Results: The results showed that those who recalled in the same environment as that in which they had learned the words recalled 40 per cent more than those recalling in a different environment.

Conclusion: They concluded that recall of information is improved if it occurs in the context in which it was learned.

🔍 RESEARCH METHODS

The Godden and Baddeley study is an example of a field experiment. An explanation of a field experiment and its advantages and disadvantages can be found in Chapter 5: Research methods and ethics – part 1, pages 71–72.

Elaboration

If we elaborate on new information it seems that we can retain it better. The reason for this could be because we process the information more deeply (levels of processing explanation) or because we create links between new information (in short-term memory) and existing information (in long-term memory).

One method of elaboration is the method of loci, which can help you remember items of unrelated information such as a shopping list, topics in revision or even the key points of a speech you have to make! The idea is that you imagine putting each item in a familiar setting, such as your home or your route to college. To remember a shopping list, for example, you could imagine your route to college and create an image of each item, such as bread going in the bank, tomatoes waiting at the traffic lights and sugar in the school playground. This example makes the link stronger by putting the item in a place with the same initial letter. To recall the information you retrace your steps, 'seeing' the items in these familiar places.

TEST YOURSELF

1   Name three differences between short-term memory and long-term memory.
2   What are the three stores outlined in the multi-store model of memory?
3   What are the two levels of processing outlined in the levels of processing model? Describe them both.
4   What is a schema?
5   What did Bartlett do in the 'war of the ghosts' experiment?
6   In interference theory, what are the two types of forgetting? What is the difference between them?
7   In the Loftus study, what were the two verbs that were used in the questions put to participants?
8   Which verb resulted in participants estimating a faster speed of the car?
9   Is eyewitness testimony reliable?

CHAPTER 2

Non-verbal communication

What you need to know for the examination:

- Distinctions between non-verbal communication and verbal communication, including paralinguistics (the vocal features that accompany speech, including tone of voice, emphasis and intonation)
- Types of non-verbal communication, including:
  ○ Functions of eye contact (Argyle, 1975) – regulating the flow of information in conversation, providing feedback and expressing emotions, including pupil dilation
  ○ Facial expressions – categories of facial expression (surprise, happiness, fear, anger, sadness, disgust); facial expressions and the hemispheres of the brain (Sackeim, 1978)
  ○ Body language – posture (including postural echo, open and closed postures), gestures and touch
- Description and evaluation of studies of non-verbal communication and verbal communication, for example the work of Argyle, Alkema and Gilmore (1971)
- Personal space – factors that affect personal space including cultural norms, sex differences, individual differences and status
- Description and evaluation of studies that affect personal space
- Contemporary practical implications of studies of non-verbal communication and their benefits and drawbacks

Figure 3.1 Communication doesn't always have to be verbal!

KEY TERMS

Non-verbal communication (NVC) – The process of sending and receiving messages through gesture, body language, posture, facial expressions and eye contact.

Verbal communication – speaking directly, using sentences etc.

Paralinguistics – the vocal features that accompany speech, including tone of voice, emphasis and intonation.

As humans, we are always communicating with other people, whether it be verbally or non-verbally. Non-verbal communication is a process of communication in which we send and receive messages without using words. It can be through gesture (using our hands), body language, posture, facial expressions and eye contact.

ACTIVITY

For each of the examples of non-verbal communication, can you state how people might communicate in this form? Can you think of any examples?

- Gesture
- Body language
- Posture
- Facial expressions
- Eye contact.

Did you know that 55 per cent of our communication with others consists of non-verbal communication (Albert Mehrabian, 1971)?

ACTIVITY

Next time you are in a fairly busy place (for example, the school canteen) conduct a mini observation of non-verbal communication. Record your findings and feed back to your class your observations.

Having a conversation can also contain elements of non-verbal communication. The vocal features that accompany speech are known as paralinguistics. These can include:

- The tone of voice
- The emphasis and intonation (e.g. stressing certain words).

The use of paralinguistics may change the meaning of words.

We have already mentioned that non-verbal communication forms 55 per cent of communication (body language), but did you know that 38 per cent is expressed through the tone of voice (paralinguistics)? Only 7 per cent is communicated through words.

THE FUNCTIONS OF NON-VERBAL COMMUNICATION

Michael Argyle (1988) concluded there are five functions of non-verbal bodily behaviour in human communication:

- To express emotions
- To express interpersonal attitudes
- To accompany speech in managing the cues of interaction between speakers and listeners
- Presentation of one's personality
- Rituals (greetings).

The interaction of verbal and non-verbal communication to regulate the flow of conversation

When we talk to other people, non-verbal communication can interact with verbal messages to assist (regulate) the flow of conversation in a number of different ways. These are as follows:

- **Repeating** – using gestures to strengthen/repeat a verbal message, such as pointing to the object of discussion
- **Conflicting** – verbal and non-verbal messages can sometimes send conflicting messages. For example, a person expressing a statement of truth verbally while simultaneously fidgeting or avoiding eye contact may convey a mixed message to the listener
- **Complementing** – accurate interpretation of messages is made easier when non-verbal and verbal communication complement each other. Non-verbal cues can be used to reinforce the information sent, such as smiling while thanking someone
- **Substituting** – non-verbal signals can be used as a substitute for a verbal message, such as raising eyebrows instead of asking a question, or nodding the head as a sign of agreement
- **Regulating** – non-verbal behaviour also regulates our conversations. For example, touching someone's arm can signal that you want to interrupt or be the next to talk.

Eye contact

When one person looks at another, there is good evidence to suggest that we tend to concentrate on the face (Argyle, 1975), and temporary facial expressions (smiles or frowns) have been proved to be a reliable indicator of a person's mood.

Eye contact is important because it can indicate whether a person is interested, paying attention or involved in a conversation. Even subtle cues like the amount of pupil dilation can be used to assess a person's mood with considerable accuracy.

ASK YOURSELF

Can you think of a situation where you or somebody you know has emphasised certain words? Why do we do this? What effect does it have on the listener?

ASK YOURSELF

Why is eye contact important?

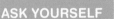

ACTIVITY

Can you think of somebody that you know who gives eye contact when talking to you, and somebody who doesn't? Can you notice the difference? How does it make you feel? Write down your thoughts.

ASK YOURSELF

Can you think of some examples of facial expressions and what they mean?

Cultural differences in the use of eye contact

Japanese people consider direct and constant eye contact a rude gesture that means a challenge. They may look down to show respect to another. In the UK, it is good manners to look at a person's eyes when they are talking.

Facial expression

Facial expression is a 'giveaway' to the thoughts that are crossing your mind but are not being expressed verbally.

ACTIVITY

In pairs, have a go at using some facial expressions and get your partner to guess what they are.

ACTIVITY

Look at the following pictures and decide what they mean. Is the person suggesting disagreement or agreement/pleasure?

Paul Ekman (1972) suggested that there were six universal facial expressions: happiness, sadness, anger, fear, surprise and disgust. This means that anybody, regardless of where they come from in the world, would recognise and be able to interpret them.

Different categories of facial expression

To match a facial expression with an emotion requires knowledge of human emotions. As babies we learn this through observing others. There are different types of facial expressions:

- Happiness – this is universally and easily recognised. When we are happy it may be interpreted as enjoyment, pleasure or friendliness. People can easily pick out a happy face from a photograph.
- Sadness – this is the opposite of happiness. Sadness may convey messages related to loss, pain, discomfort and helplessness.
- Anger – this may be seen in daily stresses like frustration. Its expression conveys messages about hostility and potential attack.
- Fear – this can convey messages about a possible threat or danger.

ACTIVITY

Look at the picture below. Can you match up the facial expression with the right picture?

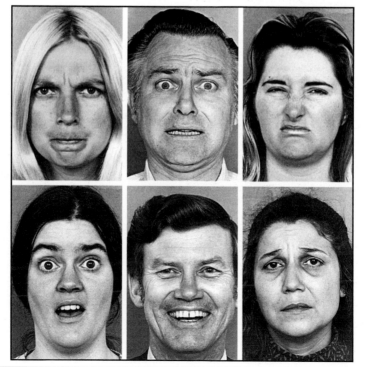

ACTIVITY

The pictures here are of a face with a mirror reversal. You need to mount the two faces on cards – note these two faces are identical but reversed.

Ask 20 people to focus on the nose of face 1 for five seconds and then rate the face for 'happiness' on a scale of one to ten. Then ask another 20 people to focus on the nose of face 2 for five seconds and rate this face for happiness. If Sackeim is correct, people should rate the second face as happier because the left side of the mouth turns up. Warning! Left-handed people should be excluded from taking part. Do you know why?

Do your findings support Sackheim's results and theory?

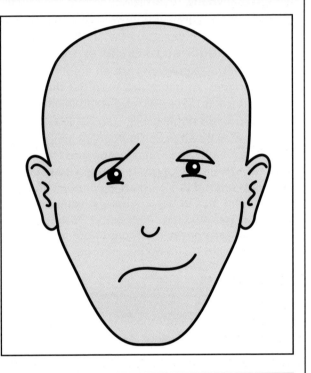

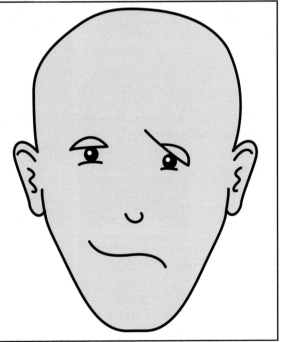

- Surprise – a brief emotional state that is the result of experiencing an unexpected relevant event. Surprise can be neutral, pleasant or unpleasant.
- Disgust – this occurs as a reaction to objects that are revolting, for example the smell of rotting fish, or if somebody has offended you.

Charles Darwin believed that facial expressions of emotion are similar among humans, regardless of culture.

H. Sackheim (1978) conducted research into how facial expressions are perceived and he suggests that the expression displayed on the left side of the face (controlled by the right hemisphere of the brain) is perceived more strongly.

Pictures of human faces posing six distinct emotions (plus a neutral expression) and their mirror reversals were split down the middle, and left-side and right-side composites were constructed. Subjects judged left-side composites as expressing emotions more intensely than right-side composites. The finding indicates hemispheric asymmetry in the control over emotional expression in the face.

Body language

Posture

The way that people hold themselves can give important information to other people.

Theodore Sarbin and C. Hardyk (1953) suggest there are a number of postures that have a fairly clear meaning for us. They are normally seen as indicators of how a person is feeling (for example, tense or relaxed).

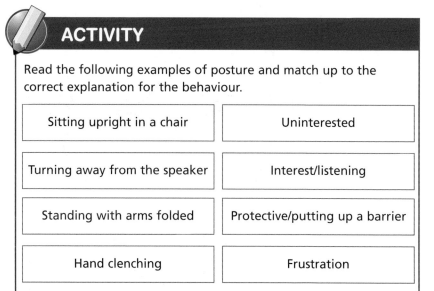

ACTIVITY

Read the following examples of posture and match up to the correct explanation for the behaviour.

Sitting upright in a chair	Uninterested
Turning away from the speaker	Interest/listening
Standing with arms folded	Protective/putting up a barrier
Hand clenching	Frustration

There are different types of posture.

The **postural echo** is when people copy each other's posture. We are likely to demonstrate this among friends. It carries the message: 'I am like you.' Successful sales people are known to use this, as are people who are flirting with one another.

An **open posture** can include any of the following: knees apart, legs stretched out, elbows away from body, hands not touching and legs uncrossed.

A **closed posture** can include: legs crossed at either knees or ankles, hands folded on lap and arms crossed.

Individuals with open body positions are perceived more positively than those with closed body positions. Individuals with open body positions are also more persuasive than those with closed body positions

ACTIVITY

With your partner, have a go at displaying both open and closed postures. Which one do you think could lead to more successful and positive behaviour?

ASK YOURSELF

Can you think of any situations where either of these postures would be used?

Knowledge of posture and how posture is perceived can be extremely helpful to professional psychologists such as counsellors. If, for instance, a couple enter into marriage counselling, or a family enters into family guidance or counselling, how they interact with one another can be expressed in body language as well as verbally. The counsellor can use this information when understanding the couple or the family and can help them to understand how they are behaving both verbally and non-verbally towards one another.

ASK YOURSELF

Can you think of any gestures that you, or somebody that you know, uses?

Gestures

A gesture is a form of non-verbal communication made with a part of the body, used instead of, or in combination with, verbal communication.

Gestures allow individuals to express a variety of feelings and thoughts, from contempt and hostility to approval and affection. Most people use gestures and body language in addition to words when they speak.

Gestures do not have universal meanings. Even simple gestures like pointing at someone can give offence if it is not done correctly. In the USA and western European countries it is very common for people to point with an extended finger, but in Asia this is considered very rude.

Gestures can take the form of a body gesture, facial gesture or a hand gesture. Some of these are listed below:

Body gestures

A body gesture known as 'the peacock' expresses superiority or domination combined with a certain degree of smug arrogance. It is performed by pushing the chest up and out at the front as well as tilting the face slightly upward.

Facial gestures

These include:

- **Eye rolling** – rotating the eyes upward, which generally signals boredom or exasperation. It can be interpreted as the equivalent of saying: 'I don't like this' or 'I think this is really stupid.'
- **Nodding** – in many cultures a nod is a gesture of confirmation, to agree with something, or to show that someone is listening or interested.
- **Head shaking** – the opposite of a nod; in many cultures it signals disagreement.

If you watch the news you can see the 'nodding' gesture put to very good use. A reporter may nod while 'listening' carefully to someone they are interviewing, giving us, the audience, the impression that they are listening intently. In fact the 'nodding' part of the film we are watching is more often than not filmed after the interview and edited in to make it seem as if the reporter is listening carefully in an interested fashion. These films of a nodding reporter are called 'noddies' in the world of television reporting and are extremely common! They are a practical use of the gesture in that they are used to make the audience understand, or at least think, that the reporter is paying careful and close attention to their interviewee.

Hand gestures

These can include gestures performed by one or two hands. Can you think of any examples?

Gordon Brown (the prime minister at the time of writing) uses hand gestures when he speaks. He holds his right hand in front of him with the thumb raised. Some regard this as a sort of barrier placed in front of him. When he wants to explain that something is developing or moving forward, he moves his hand forwards at the same time, which depicts the movement of a barrier of some kind. This is amazingly similar to the hand gestures used by the prime minister who came before him, Tony Blair. It has been suggested that Mr Brown uses these hand gestures on purpose, and has possibly been taught to do so – a psychological trick to help us link the two prime ministers together, and provide a smooth movement from one to the next.

KEY STUDY

Argyle, Alkema and Gilmour (1971)

Aim: To investigate the communication of friendly and hostile attitudes by verbal and non-verbal signals

Method: Three verbal statements, either friendly, hostile or neutral in content, were delivered to participants in one of three non-verbal styles:

- Friendly – soft tone, open posture, smiling
- Hostile – harsh tone, closed posture, frowning
- Neutral – displaying neither friendly nor hostile cues.

Participants then rated how friendly or hostile they perceived the messages to be.

Results: The non-verbal message greatly outweighed the content of the verbal message.

Conclusion: Michael Argyle, F. Alkema and R. Gilmour concluded that non-verbal communication was 12.5 times more powerful than language in the friendly/hostile dimension. The implications of this research are clear. Knowledge of how someone feels by their tone and appearance is useful in working out how we might react to them. This is very useful in situations where people are often emotional. For instance, the police often need to interpret non-verbal behaviour so that they can react to it quickly.

PERSONAL SPACE

Edward Hall (1959) defined personal space as an 'emotionally charged bubble of space which surrounds each individual'.

It is an invisible bubble that surrounds us and is carried with us when we move. If anyone enters our bubble they invade our personal space. Hall (1966) identified four distances of personal space.

ACTIVITY

In pairs, work out your own personal space. Take turns to walk towards your partner until they say: 'Stop.' This will indicate their area of personal space.

Personal space distance	Size of distance	Social use
Intimate distance	0–0.5 m	Used for an intimate relationship. Can also be used in social situations such as shaking hands.
Personal distance	0.5–1.5 m	Used by close friends and acquaintances and allows conversations to take place.
Social distance	1.5–4.0 m	For more formal situations, such as people who are acquaintances or in business transactions.
Public distance	Over 4.0 m	The distance between one person and a group, for example at a lecture or at a concert.

ACTIVITY

Imagine you had to write a description of personal space. What happens when people invade your personal space? How does it make you feel? Does it depend on the person as to how close they can get to you? Write down your answers.

ACTIVITY

Next time you are in a public place, have a look at the various people who are there. Can you tell from the distance that they are keeping from other people they are talking to as to who those people are (for example, boyfriend/girlfriend, work colleague etc.)?

Research into the invasion of personal space

Felipe and Sommer (1966) conducted two field experiments. One took place in the grounds of a large mental institution: when a man was sitting alone on a bench, someone came and sat down next to him, sitting 15cm away. If the participant moved along the bench, the 'invader' followed. Observers noted the length of time before the participants left and compared them with a control group (males sitting alone) who were watched from a distance. The results showed that 20 per cent had left after one minute (compared to none of the controls) and 50 per cent after nine minutes (compared to 8 per cent of the controls).

Felipe and Sommer (1966) also conducted a study in a library using people who were sitting by themselves. Results showed that when an 'invader' sat in the next chair and moved it closer, 70 per cent of the participants had left their seats after 30 minutes, whereas only 13 per cent left when the participants allowed a gap of one chair between them.

This study also showed that many participants also changed the angle of their chair, pulled in their elbows and used books or other objects as barriers. People also change their body position, leaning away from the invader or turning the angle of their body to present more of a barrier.

There are practical implications for this research. Knowledge of how people like to be seated is important in the design of public spaces, such as libraries. If it is our intention to help people feel as comfortable as possible when working in groups together, then knowing how to organise the space is very important. For instance, arranging a classroom in tables of six may be better than arranging it in tables of eight if we hope to encourage conversation in a class. Arranging chairs in long rows, such as at a cinema or theatre, is good if we want to discourage group discussion and encourage attention.

ACTIVITY

Do you think that there are cultural differences in personal space? Why do you think this is so?

Cultural differences in personal space

Hall (1966) conducted cross-cultural research and found that in cultures with high 'sensory contact' (such as French, Greek and Arabic) personal distances are much closer than in low sensory contact cultures (such as American, English and Swiss). Because of these differences, someone standing too far away could cause offence in one culture, and standing too close cause discomfort in another.

J. Baxter (1970) showed that personal distances varied according to the setting. African-Americans interacted more closely in indoor settings, whereas Mexican-Americans were closest in outdoor settings.

As we live in a multicultural society, the practical implications of this research are very important. Knowing how different cultures prefer to interact is important when we interact with cultures different to our own, and this is happening more and more. Ensuring that a colleague from another culture is comfortable is a useful way of building a good relationship with them.

Gender differences in personal space

There are several differences between the personal space of men and of women.

J. Fisher and D. Byrne (1975) arranged for a confederate to invade the space of a person while they were sitting alone in a library. Invaders were either male or female, and sat next to or opposite the subject. After a few minutes the invader left and a student (another confederate) then came over and asked for the participant's impressions. These were:

- Male participants disliked the invader who sat opposite, but did not mind when the invader sat by them
- Female participants disliked the invader sitting next to them, but did not mind the invader sitting opposite.

The implications of this research are clear. When men and women interact, each prefers a different seating position. This might be of use where people are required to meet professionally. For instance, if a male manager is discussing something with a female employee they may choose to sit in a position that would make the employee feel comfortable.

In social situations, such as parties or social gatherings, where someone sits relative to us may provide us with information about whether they feel comfortable and in control. Where a man or woman chooses to sit in a situation like this can tell us quite a lot about how they may feel about one another!

Status differences in personal space

The larger amount of space claimed by rich and high-status people in a community is clearly evident in their larger homes, gardens, cars, garages, offices, and so on. The lower in status and rank a person is, the less space they command and control in every aspect of their life.

TEST YOURSELF

1 What is the difference between verbal and non-verbal communication?
2 What are the different types of non-verbal communication?
3 Why is eye contact important?
4 What did Sackheim suggest in his research?
5 What are the different types of posture?
6 What is a gesture?

CHAPTER 3

Development of personality

WHAT YOU NEED TO KNOW FOR THE EXAMINATION

What you need to know for the examination:

- The definition of personality, including temperament
- Description and evaluation of studies of temperament, including the work of Thomas (1977), Buss and Plomin (1984) and Kagan (1991)
- Eysenck's type theory (1952) including extroversion, introversion and neuroticism
- Personality scales, including EPI (1964) and EPQ (1965)
- Evaluation of Eysenck's type theory
- Antisocial personality disorder, its characteristics (DSMIV 2008) and causes, including:
  - Biological causes – the role of the amygdala, including the work of Raine (2000)
  - Situational causes – including the work of Farrington (1995) and Elander (2000)
- Description and evaluation of studies of the causes of antisocial personality disorder
- Implications of research into antisocial personality disorder

ASK YOURSELF

How would you describe your personality? Is your personality the same as anybody else's? Where does your personality come from? Is your personality fixed or can it change?

We will consider the above points and lots more within this chapter.

PERSONALITY AND TEMPERAMENT

To start, a definition of personality as explained by Richard Gross is: 'those relatively stable and enduring aspects of individuals which distinguish them from other people, making them unique, but which at the same time allow people to be compared with each other'.

Our personality is what defines us as a person. The way we think, interact with other people and behave are all individual to us as a person.

Temperament refers to our inborn personality traits. The different ways infants interact with and react to their environment and experiences are reflective of their temperament. Temperament:

- Is present from early childhood
- Is determined by inborn (genetic) mechanisms
- Can change due to maturation (as we mature) and due to the life experiences that we go through.

A number of studies have been conducted to test temperament.

RESEARCH INTO TEMPERAMENT

Thomas (1977) conducted a longitudinal study into personality and temperament. A longitudinal study is one that is conducted over a number of years. It enables the researcher to track developments and changes in a particular person or group of people.

KEY STUDY

Thomas (1977)

Aim: To conduct a longitudinal study into personality and temperament.

Method: The study actually started in 1956, using babies that were between the ages of two and three months. They were reassessed at various intervals between infancy and adulthood. Thomas used parental ratings at first and then other methods as the children got older. Once the children had been observed and the parents interviewed on several occasions, Thomas came up with a list of nine categories of behaviour, including categories such as 'quality of mood', 'attention span' and 'distractibility'.

Results/Conclusion: Using all of these categories of behaviour, Thomas then suggested that there were three types of temperament: easy temperament, difficult temperament and slow-to-warm-up temperament.

1 **Easy temperament** – defined by high scores on regularity, approach, adaptability, mild or moderate intensity of reaction, and predominance of positive mood.
2 **Difficult temperament** – the opposite of easy temperament, with irregularity, withdrawal, non-adaptability, intense reactions and negative mood.
3 **Slow-to-warm-up temperament** – consists of mild negative reactions and slow adaptation to new stimuli or persons, but only mild intensity of emotional reactions and no irregularity.

Another study into temperament was conducted by Arnold Buss and Robert Plomin (1984). They defined temperament as 'traits observable by two years of age that are genetic in origin'.

Buss and Plomin developed rating scales of temperament for parents to describe their children and a self-report test for adults. There were four basic traits of temperament, described in the key study that follows.

KEY STUDY

Buss and Plomin (1984)

Aim: To see if inherited traits of temperament are evident in childhood.

Method: They developed rating scales of temperament for parents to describe their children, and a self-report test for adults.

Results/Conclusion: Buss and Plomin identified four basic traits of temperament evident in children:

1 **Emotionality** – gets upset and cries easily, is easily frightened and/or has a quick temper, is not easy-going.
2 **Activity** – always on the go from the time of waking, cannot sit still for long, fidgets at meals, prefers active games to quiet ones.
3 **Sociability** – likes to be with others, makes friends easily, prefers to play with others rather than alone, is not shy.
4 **Impulsivity** – difficulty in learning self-control and resistance to temptation, gets bored easily, goes from toy to toy quickly.

Jerome Kagan and Nancy Snidman (1991) provide a theory that one particular personality trait – shyness – comes about because a part of the brain, the amygdala, is overactive. The amygdala is responsible for our emotion of fear; an overactive amygdala may result in nervousness, which may well result in a person being shy. In their research Kagan and Snidman found that shy children showed fear-like responses to new stimuli. These included a faster beating heart and widened (dilated) pupils in their eyes. These reactions are controlled partly by the amygdala, so it was concluded that they had an overactive amygdala.

KEY STUDY

Kagan and Snidman (1991)

Aim: To compare inhibited and less inhibited young children.

Method: They compared the behaviour of emotionally reserved (shy) children with the behaviour of sociable (non-shy) children.

Results/Conclusion: Kagan and Snidman reported that:

1 About 10 per cent of children tested were emotionally reserved and shy.
2 Infants with high levels of motor activity and crying were more fearful of new or novel events and, when facing new events, their muscles tightened, their pupils dilated (became wider) and their hearts pumped faster and harder.
3 The nervousness (shyness) remained as the child developed: children of nine months, tested again at 14 months showed the same behaviour.

EXAM STYLE QUESTIONS

Describe and evaluate one study in which temperament was investigated. Include in your answer the method used, the results obtained, the conclusion drawn and an evaluation point.

Figure 3.1 Hans Eysenck

EYSENCK'S TYPE THEORY

Many theories have been put forward to try and explain personality. One of the most famous theories was developed by Hans Eysenck (1952) and is known as the 'type theory'.

Eysenck was interested in personality in general and believed in the idea that personality consisted of permanent traits or characteristics. The research that Eysenck conducted led him to suggest that there were three important traits in a person's personality: extroversion, introversion and neuroticism.

Extroversion (the person displaying this behaviour would be known as an extrovert) refers to an outgoing nature and a high level of activity within a person. **Introversion** (the person displaying this behaviour would be known as an introvert) is the opposite and refers to somebody who prefers to do things on their own and not in a crowd. **Neuroticism** (the person displaying this behaviour would be known as 'neurotic') refers to a nature full of anxiety, guilt and worry.

Personality scales

There are different ways to measure personality. The original questionnaire was the Maudsley Medical Questionnaire, which only measured neuroticism. This was then replaced by the Maudsley Personality Inventory, which measured both extroversion and neuroticism.

ASK YOURSELF

What might be a problem with using questionnaires to measure personality?

Eysenck developed two scales: the Eysenck Personality Inventory (EPI, 1964) and the Eysenck Personality Questionnaire (EPQ, 1975). The EPI added a lie scale. This measures a person's tendency to give answers that are socially desirable (which makes them look good).

How do personality scales work? They all have yes/no items, so the data is quantitative (numerical) and can be analysed in order to make comparisons.

Questions that could be used to measure personality would be something like:

- Do you long for excitement? – this would measure extroversion
- Are you an outgoing person? – this too would measure extroversion
- Do you sometimes feel anxious? – this would measure neuroticism
- Are you a moody person? – this too would measure neuroticism.

ACTIVITY

Have a go at devising your own questionnaire using Eysenck's ideas.

⚖️ **EVALUATION BOX**

The scales are well respected and accepted as research tools. Eysenck used to give the questionnaires to groups of people who are known to differ on the dimensions in question. Even though the questionnaires are not meant to diagnose neuroticism, we would still expect diagnosed neurotics to score very high on this compared to a control group of non-neurotics.

So far we have considered what personality is, how it develops and how it can be measured.

We now need to look at what happens when a person's personality can have very negative effects on society – this is called antisocial personality disorder.

Figure 3.2 Disregarding the safety of self or others can be part of antisocial personality disorder

ANTISOCIAL PERSONALITY DISORDER

There has been a great deal of research in the last decade or so into antisocial personality disorder.

The essential features of the diagnosis according to DSMIV 2008 are a pervasive pattern of disregard for and violation of the rights of others that begins in childhood or early adulthood and continues into adulthood.

Three or more of the following behaviours are required for a diagnosis of antisocial personality disorder:

1 Failure to conform to social norms with respect to lawful behaviours, as indicated by repeatedly performing acts that are grounds for arrest.
2 Deceitfulness – repeated lying, conning others for personal profit or pleasure.
3 Irritability or aggressiveness (for example physical fights or assaults).

KEY TERM

Antisocial personality disorder (APD) – a pervasive pattern of disregard for and violation of the rights of others that begins in childhood or early adulthood and continues into adulthood.

4 Lack of remorse as indicated by stealing from others.
5 Failure to plan ahead.

There have been many explanations put forward as to the causes of antisocial personality disorder. We will consider one explanation from a biological perspective and another from a psychosocial perspective.

Biological explanations of the causes of the antisocial personality disorder

The biological perspective suggests that there are biological causes of our behaviour, such as genetics, brain structure, hormones etc. Research suggests that one part of the brain, the amygdala, may be responsible for the development of antisocial personality disorder. The amygdala is a part of the brain that is primarily responsible for learning from one's mistakes and is responsible for human responses to sad and fearful facial expressions.

It has been shown that in cases of antisocial personality disorder, the amygdala is smaller than it is in non-antisocial personality disorder people, and responds less to the happy, sad or fearful facial expressions of others. This reduced response may explain the lack of empathy that antisocial personality disorder individuals tend to have with the feelings, rights and suffering of others.

Adrian Raine (2000) wanted to investigate whether criminals' brains were any different from law-abiding brains. He wanted to find out if people who had committed murder and who had pleaded not guilty by reason of insanity showed any evidence of brain abnormalities.

His sample consisted of 41 criminals (39 males and 2 females) who were all charged with murder and who were pleading not guilty by reason of insanity. He also had a control group to be used as a comparison with the experimental group. The people in the experimental group were all diagnosed with schizophrenia (six of the criminals), head injury or personality disorders. Those in the experimental group were matched by age, sex and diagnosis to those in the control group. For example, the people with a personality disorder were matched with people in the control group having a personality disorder, but those in the control group had not committed murder.

Once they had been matched, all of the participants in both groups were prevented from taking their medication (for their illness) for two weeks prior to the investigation. This was so that the researchers could rule out the effects of the drugs as a variable that might affect the accuracy (validity) of the results.

On the day of the experiment, all participants were injected with a glucose tracker. They then took part in a target-recognition task for 32 minutes. They were then given a PET scan (a type of brain scan

ASK YOURSELF

Why was it important to match them on the same criteria?

that measures brain activity). The researchers were comparing the level and location of brain activity in the left and right hemispheres in the brain.

Compared with the control group, participants in the offending group were found to have:

- Less activity in the left hemisphere and more in the right hemisphere
- Less activity in the prefrontal area of the brain
- Abnormal asymmetries in amygdala.

So, what does this mean? The difference in the amygdala supports the theory that violence is due to unusual emotional responses such as a lack of fear. The difference in the prefrontal cortex may be important because this area of the brain is where rational thinking takes place.

Therefore, individuals who plead not guilty by reason of insanity did have significantly different levels of activity in the brain, and these differences might have led them to become violent.

This is an interesting piece of research, but it does *not* suggest that all violent people have abnormalities in the brain.

EVALUATION BOX

- A small sample was used (41 murderers from California); findings cannot be generalised as this is not a representative sample.
- The control and experimental groups were matched for age, sex and illness, allowing for a valid comparison. This means that it would be clear to see if there were any differences between the groups.
- The medication was controlled, ruling out the possible effect that this could have on the brain activity at the time of the investigation. If the medication hadn't been controlled, it could have led researchers to gain invalid data.
- From these findings we cannot suggest that violence is determined by biology alone; there must be other factors that lead a person to become violent.
- The research is correlational – this means that there is a relationship between the two variables, in this case criminal behaviour and damage to the amygdala. However, we cannot assume cause and effect; there may be other variables that may affect violent behaviour.

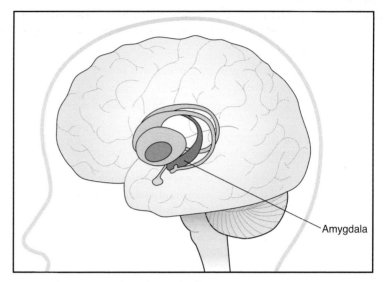

Figure 3.3 The amygdala is found in the frontal lobe of the brain

Situational explanations of the causes of antisocial personality disorder

Raine's study may support the idea that our personality is determined by our biology, but we cannot rule out the role that psychosocial factors play (psychosocial means a combination of psychological and social factors).

David Farrington (1995) conducted longitudinal research funded by the Home Office to determine whether adult antisocial personality disorder could be predicted from psychosocial factors present during childhood.

He conducted the 'Cambridge Study in Delinquent Development'. His sample consisted of 411 south London males aged between eight and 10 years. They were looking for psychosocial risk factors as a predictor for antisocial personality disorder. They discovered that the following factors were important:

- Convicted parent
- Belonging to a large family
- Being of low intelligence
- Child-rearing factors (for example, young mother and disrupted family).

To gather this data Farrington would have used methods such as interviews with the children and their families, and IQ tests.

He concluded that the risk factors were pretty accurate. Nearly half of the boys with convicted parents at age 10 were antisocial by the age of 32. Over 60 per cent of the boys who were at very high risk at ages eight to 10 were antisocial by the age of 32.

This research supports the idea that the environment can also play a role in the development of personality, including the development of antisocial personality disorder.

Figure 3.4 Belonging to a large family can be a risk factor for antisocial personality disorder

EVALUATION BOX

- A large sample was used (411 males).
- Only males were used in the sample, meaning the findings can't be generalised to females. Females may behave differently from males, so this concept cannot explain female behaviour.
- The sample only consisted of males from south London. This means that it cannot be generalised to people who live in different areas (it is not a representative sample).
- The risk factors were good predictors in the development of antisocial personality disorder; however, the factors were not 100 per cent accurate, so there must be other factors that are important in the development of antisocial personality disorder.
- Not all people who have these factors in their life will go on to develop antisocial personality disorder.
- A longitudinal study is a good way of seeing changes and development in a person over time; however, participants may drop out of the study (they may choose to withdraw, or they may leave the area), which could lead to inconclusive findings.

James Elander (2000) conducted research into antisocial behaviour. He analysed the psychiatric and forensic histories of 13 individuals, all of whom had committed crimes after the age of 22. He noticed that there was evidence of minor juvenile delinquency in 12 of the 13 participants. Their childhood had consisted of antisocial behaviour and there was evidence of mental illness. Juvenile delinquency and mental illness were identified as risk factors. Elander concluded that these risk factors had contributed to the apparent late onset of criminality.

EXAM STYLE QUESTIONS

Describe and evaluate one study in which antisocial personality disorder was investigated. Include in your answer the method used in the study, the results obtained, the conclusion drawn and an evaluation of the study.

IMPLICATIONS OF RESEARCH INTO ANTISOCIAL PERSONALITY DISORDER

The practical implications of research into antisocial personality disorder are potentially extremely important. If someone with no personality disorder or psychological illness of any kind commits a crime, they will be punished with prison or fines. If, however, someone is found to have an antisocial personality disorder, then many believe that punishment is not the correct course of action. Since the person is psychologically ill, they may benefit more from treatment than punishment. Nevertheless, they often find themselves in prison or in secure hospitals, which restricts their freedom.

Research tells us that antisocial personality disorder may arise for a number of reasons. Raine (2000) tells us that it may be genetic or biological, caused by the type of brain the person has; Farrington (1995) tells us that it may be something to do with the environment in which we develop. Whatever the cause, the personalities of those with antisocial personality disorder have been formed and they have great difficulty behaving responsibly and in a way that is acceptable to society. For this reason we need to ensure that those with antisocial personality disorder are able to find help.

We could stop them breaking the law by locking them up until they can learn to behave in an acceptable way, but many consider this to be cruel and unfair. After all, if they have a psychological illness, it is not their fault. Others, however, feel that the safest way to deal with those with antisocial personality disorder who are, after all, often extremely dangerous, is to keep them in secure hospitals.

In addition to this, research suggests that punishing people with antisocial personality disorder seems to have little or no effect (Michael Passer *et al.*, 2008). Whereas many people would respond to a prison sentence by not wanting to offend again and so return to prison, those with antisocial personality disorder lack a feeling of fear and anxiety, so the threat of punishment does not seem to deter them in any way. This means that careful monitoring and treatment or secure hospitalisation is the only response society can make.

TEST YOURSELF

1 Define what psychologists mean by personality.
2 Define what psychologists mean by temperament.
3 What were the two different types of questionnaires used by Eysenck?
4 Write a question that could assess if a person was an extrovert according to Eysenck.
5 Write a question that could assess if a person was an introvert according to Eysenck.
6 What is meant by antisocial personality disorder?
7 What did Raine conclude in his research findings?
8 What did Farrington conclude in his research findings?
9 State the difference between a biological and a situational risk factor, and give an example of each.

CHAPTER 4

Stereotyping, prejudice and discrimination

WHAT YOU NEED TO KNOW FOR THE EXAMINATION

What you need to know for the examination:
- Definitions of stereotyping, prejudice and discrimination
- Stereotyping as oversimplification, leading to positive and negative evaluations
- Description and evaluation of studies of prejudice and discrimination, including the work of Adorno (authoritarian personality, and the F-scale), Tajfel (in-groups and out-groups) and Sherif (Robbers Cave), and inter-group conflict

- Explanations of prejudice and discrimination
- Ways of reducing prejudice and discrimination, using evidence from studies including the work of Sherif (1961), Aronson (1978), Elliot (1977) and Harwood (2003)
- Evaluation of ways of reducing prejudice and discrimination
- Contemporary practical implications of research into stereotyping, prejudice and discrimination, and their benefits and drawbacks

STEREOTYPING

A **stereotype** is a shared belief about the characteristics of those who belong to a particular social or physical category.

We may identify them on the basis of visible cues, such as race, gender, physical shape or clothing, or less visible information such as job, sexual orientation or religion. By stereotyping we assume that the person has a whole range of characteristics and abilities, which we assume all members of that group have. An example of a commonly held stereotype is that students are lazy!

KEY TERM

Stereotype – a shared belief about the characteristics of those who belong to a particular social or physical category.

ACTIVITY

Can you think of any more examples of stereotypes?

Figure 4.1 Stereotypical English and French men (in terms of their dress sense)

ACTIVITY

Imagine you are reading a newspaper and the main headline is that two girls, aged seven, have been expelled from school for aggressive behaviour. Why do you think this would cause more controversy than if it were about two boys of the same age?

Stereotypes are often used in a negative sense.

ACTIVITY

Imagine you are on holiday. You are in the swimming pool with your friends/family and you start to splash each other. Another holidaymaker who is sitting at the edge of the pool, who is foreign but speaks very good English, does not look happy at you splashing each other. You hear her say to her friend: 'Typical English.'

Is this fair? Are you going to be treated fairly? Where might this stereotype have come from?

How can this lead to problems with the use of stereotypes? Is she treating you as an individual?

In a situation such as the one outlined in the previous activity, it is likely that you would be treated in a negative way, and you would not be treated as an individual. These are disadvantages of the use of stereotypes, and they can lead us to think things about people that might not be true. Some more disadvantages of stereotypes include:

- They are usually oversimplified
- They lead us to make assumptions about others when we know very little about them
- They affect what we remember and forget about other people
- They lead us to view members of out-groups (people who don't belong to our group) in a negative way, leading to prejudice and discrimination.

However, stereotypes can have their advantages too:

- One advantage of a stereotype is that it can enable us to respond quickly to situations because we may have had a similar experience before
- Using stereotypes is a simple way of organising and remembering information about other people
- It reduces the amount of cognitive effort we need to make (for example, thinking)
- They help us to interpret unknown information about someone else
- They provide us with a sense of belonging to a group, because of our shared beliefs about people in other groups.

Holding a stereotype about a person can lead to prejudice, and can allow the person being stereotyped to be treated unfairly. This leads us on to the next section: prejudice and discrimination.

EXAM STYLE QUESTIONS

Read the conversation below:

Boy A: I was speaking to my granddad the other day on the telephone and told him that I was going to start supporting my favourite football team and going to watch them play. He said he was worried that I would change as a person.
Boy B: Why did he say that, do you think?
Boy A: Because he said he thought that I was going to turn into a football hooligan.

What is meant by stereotyping? Refer to the example above in your explanation.

ACTIVITY

Can you pick out the positive stereotypes and the negative stereotypes from the list below?

- All black people are great basketball players
- All immigrants in the UK are on benefits
- All Latinos dance well.

PREJUDICE AND DISCRIMINATION

Prejudice can be defined as an attitude, which is usually negative, towards a particular group of people, based on characteristics that are assumed to be common to all members of the group. Although prejudice can be positive or negative, psychologists have been much more concerned with its negative aspects because of their damaging effects. For example, a person may be prejudiced towards a person of a particular race.

People might express negative attitudes towards others because they are of a different religion, or a different culture. People might make assumptions about others based on their sexual orientation, their age, their physical appearance or their lifestyle.

Discrimination can be defined as treating people unfavourably on the basis of their membership of a particular group. Discrimination is usually, but not always, the behaviour resulting from prejudice. Discrimination includes ignoring someone, keeping a distance, using an unfriendly tone of voice, showing preference to others over them, harassing or even attacking them.

The difference between prejudice and discrimination

Prejudice can be seen as the negative attitude and discrimination as the resultant behaviour.

A prejudiced person may not act on their belief or attitude; for example, a person can be prejudiced towards a person or a person from a particular group, but not discriminate against them. An example of prejudice and discrimination that you might know from studying history would be the Nazis' mass murder of Jews during World War II.

ACTIVITY

Can you identify the prejudice and discrimination in the example of the Nazis and the Jews?

ASK YOURSELF

How do you think prejudice would affect a person who was on the receiving end of it?

KEY TERMS

Prejudice – an attitude, which is usually negative, towards a particular group of people, based on characteristics that are assumed to be common to all members of the group.

Discrimination – treating people unfavourably on the basis of their membership of a particular group.

Figure 4.2 The Jews were subject to prejudice and discrimination by the Nazis during World War II

EXPLANATIONS OF AND RESEARCH INTO PREJUDICE AND DISCRIMINATION

One explanation for why people may be prejudiced towards others was put forward by Theodor Adorno (1950). He suggested that prejudice occurred as a result of a person's personality, and that a certain personality type could lead a person to become prejudiced. Adorno *et al.* tested this idea by interviewing former Nazi soldiers at the end of World War II.

KEY STUDY

Adorno *et al.* (1950)

Aim: To test the idea that a person may be prejudiced towards somebody else because of their personality.

Method: They interviewed hundreds of former Nazi soldiers. They developed a personality scale as part of this research known as the F-scale (F stands for fascist), which they used to measure responses to a series of weighted questions.

Results: Adorno and his colleagues found a particular pattern of personality characteristics, which they called the authoritarian personality. Those with an authoritarian personality tended to be:

- Hostile to (negative towards) those who are of inferior status (for example, those who were beneath them in terms of obedience) but obedient towards those of a higher status
- Fairly rigid in their opinions (sticking with the same beliefs and opinions)
- Not willing to accept any new ideas or new situations.

KEY STUDY – (continued)

Conclusion: Adorno concluded that these characteristics make those who have them likely to categorise others readily into 'us' and 'them' groups, seeing their own group as superior and treating people of a different group in a negative way.

RESEARCH METHODS

The Adorno study is an example of an interview – a description of the features and its strengths and limitations can be found in Chapter 10: Research methods and ethics – part 2, pages 178–179.

This research also indicated that those people with an authoritarian personality were more likely to have had a very strict upbringing. Adorno claimed that these people experienced hostility (negative feelings) towards their parents that they were unable to express. This hostility was directed onto safer targets, namely those who were weaker and unable to hurt them, leading to them holding prejudiced views and discriminating against them.

EVALUATION BOX

There are several criticisms of Adorno's explanation. His identification of child-rearing style does not appear to be widely applicable, because not all prejudiced people had harsh parents, and some prejudiced people show few features of the authoritarian personality. Also, he found only a correlation between child-rearing style and the authoritarian personality.

The authoritarian personality also fails to explain *why* many people are prejudiced, nor does it explain why we are prejudiced against certain groups rather than others.

EXAM STYLE QUESTIONS

What is a correlation?
State one advantage and one disadvantage of using a correlation.

It seems we need to take account of some aspects of our social setting to explain these points.

Social identity theory

Earlier in this chapter we looked at stereotyping and we noted the ease with which we categorise people into our own group (the in-group) and the other group (the out-group). Henri Tajfel (1971) called this **social categorisation** and it is the first step in the stereotyping process. He argued that we stress or single out the differences between our group and the out-group.

Consider the following example:

At the local high school, which is renowned for its sporting achievements, students are categorised as either 'sporty' or 'non-sporty'. Alex just doesn't enjoy doing anything like sport, but wants to be part of the 'sporty' crowd because they get invited to all of the parties and have a 'cool' reputation among the students.

ACTIVITY

Is Alex part of the in-group or the out-group? How might this lead to a stereotype? How would this affect the way he was treated? Write down your answers.

So, if we use the example of Alex above to demonstrate what Tajfel said, there are differences between the in-group and the out-group, and these are being stressed or singled out.

ACTIVITY

What 'in-group' do you belong to? Who is the 'out-group'? What are the benefits of belonging to an 'in-group'?

KEY TERMS

Self-esteem – how we think and feel about ourselves.

Self-image – how you see yourself and how you believe others see you.

Tajfel proposed that the groups we are part of – our psychology class, football team, neighbourhood and so on – are an important source of pride and self-esteem.

The groups that we belong to give us our **social identity**: a sense of belonging in the social world.

In order to increase our self-image, we enhance the status of the groups to which we belong. For example, research shows that we think that members of our own group are more attractive and intelligent than those in the out-group. We also judge our group in circumstances where it is successful and tend to dismiss situations in which it does badly.

For example, Jackie belongs to the 'trendy gang' at school. Jackie and the other members of her group have very high self-esteem and a very positive self-image as they believe that they are beautiful and they think that everybody else believes this. They are known to bully some of the girls who don't follow the fashion as they do, however, and are nasty to them about their clothes. Jackie and her friends don't believe that they are doing anything wrong when confronted about their bullying.

Figure 4.3 An example of in-groups and out-groups in the film *Grease*

In real life we tend to raise the value of our own group but we do not necessarily play down others. So, although we differentiate between the in-group and the out-group, we do not necessarily have negative feelings towards the out-group. It's just that we stress the differences between 'us' and 'them'.

Gill (1980) conducted research to find out the kind of reasons people gave for their successes and failures.

She asked female basketball players what they thought was responsible for their wins and losses. Results showed that players said their successes were due to their own team's ability, but their failures were blamed on the other team. Gill concluded that people give reasons for their failure that protect their self-esteem. However, there was no evidence of playing down the other team.

Tajfel's explanation has considered prejudice as being due to competition that exists between various groups in society (in-groups and out-groups). This may be political or economic competition, and is most intense when resources are limited.

For instance, when jobs are scarce there may be an increase in prejudice towards minority groups, or when one group gains political power and uses it to benefit its own members at the expense of others. These types of circumstances can be explained by the idea of **inter-group conflict** or by **scapegoating**.

ACTIVITY

Can you think of any examples of when scapegoating has occurred?

Muzafer Sherif *et al.* (1961) put forward an inter-group conflict explanation (when people who belong to the same group experience some sort of conflict). He argued that inter-group conflict occurs when two groups are in competition for scarce resources. This argument was based on the results of a field experiment conducted by Sherif and his colleagues.

KEY STUDY

Sherif *et al.* (1961)

Aim: To investigate the idea that inter-group conflict occurs when two groups are in competition for the same thing.

Method: They observed the behaviour of 12-year-old boys who were attending a summer camp at the Robbers Cave State Park in Oklahoma. The 22 participants were not known to each other and all were white, psychologically well-adjusted and from stable, middle-class homes.

They were randomly assigned to two groups but neither was aware of the other's existence. For a few days, normal summer-camp activities took place and both groups quickly established their own culture.

A series of inter-group contests was then devised by the counsellors, with the group winning the series getting a silver cup. In addition, situations were devised in which one group gained at the expense of the other; for example, one group was delayed getting to a picnic and when they arrived the other group had eaten most of the food.

Results: Hostility quickly arose, and the groups attacked each other. Each group became more united, and the more aggressive boys became leaders.

The next stage in the study was to reduce prejudice by increasing social contact in a non-confrontational way. For instance, they all ate together and went to see a film. However, this was not effective, and it was not until the final stage that hostility was eliminated.

Conclusion: Sherif concluded that competition increases both the unity within the groups and each group's hostility towards other groups.

RESEARCH METHODS

The study above is an example of a field experiment – a description of a field experiment and its strengths and weaknesses can be found in Chapter 5: Research methods and ethics – part 1, pages 71–72.

EVALUATION BOX

- The study was a field experiment, which means it has **high ecological validity**. As a result of this, it should be expected that more natural behaviour will occur (compared with a laboratory experiment).
- The sample can be criticised and therefore cannot be generalised to real life because the research only used 12-year-old, white, middle-class boys (unlikely to reflect rival inner-city gangs or rival football supporters, for example). Also, girls were not used, so the sample can be regarded as being biased.
- **Ethical issues** must be considered. The participants were deceived, as they did not know the true aim of the study (however, the deception was necessary). Also, participants were not protected from physical and psychological harm.

EXAM STYLE QUESTIONS

Describe and evaluate one study in which prejudice and discrimination were investigated. Include in your answer the method used in the study, the results obtained, the conclusion drawn and an evaluation of the study.

EXAM STYLE QUESTIONS

Using your knowledge of psychology, give one explanation for prejudice/discrimination.

REDUCING PREJUDICE AND DISCRIMINATION

So far we have highlighted the fact that prejudice is the negative attitude and discrimination is the resultant behaviour. Most forms of discrimination are illegal in the UK. Below we consider some strategies for reducing prejudice and discrimination that have been investigated by psychologists.

Social contact

If prejudice and discrimination are based on a lack of knowledge about members of others groups, increasing the contact between members of these groups should give people more information about others, and thus break down stereotypes. However, as Sherif *et al.* (1961) found in the Robbers Cave study, it is not enough to simply bring people together.

Figure 4.4 This sign was frequently seen in America when Martin Luther King was trying to fight for black people to have equal rights to white people

In the 1970s Elliot Aronson noted that there had always been contact between black and white Americans, yet it had not reduced prejudice and discrimination. He argued that because white people saw black workers doing only menial jobs, contact merely reinforced their stereotypes and prejudice. Research shows that the more effective ways of reducing prejudice and discrimination through social contact are:

- When those experiencing prejudice and discrimination are of higher status (for example in a place of work, or in society in general) than the discriminator. Research suggests that when members of two groups are in contact, it is the higher-status members who dominate – they tend to initiate things and be listened to by others, and their views are more likely to be followed. If the members of both groups are of equal status, it is not enough to 'tip the balance' in favour of those experiencing discrimination

- When there is social support for reducing prejudice and discrimination, such as laws making discrimination illegal, social norms of toleration and respect for others.

Figure 4.5 Evelyn Glennie is deaf, so she is a member of a group who may experience discrimination. She is also a world-famous percussionist, so her high status may change some people's attitudes to deaf people

Cooperation

In the Robbers Cave study Sherif found that hostility was finally eliminated when all the boys cooperated so as to achieve goals that could not be achieved unless both groups worked together. For instance, they pulled a truck back to camp in order to get there in time for lunch. After several tasks such as this, the inter-group hostility disappeared and, indeed, several boys became good friends with boys in the other group. Sherif concluded that cooperation could reduce inter-group conflict.

However, the success of this strategy is probably due to the superficial nature of the prejudice and discrimination that Sherif's study created. The conflict was artificial, as was the difference between the groups. When the groups worked together the boys would have seen the other white, middle-class boys as similar, and they would have easily formed a new group with a common goal.

KEY STUDY

Aronson *et al.* (1978)

Aim: Aronson and his colleagues were called in by a Texas school to devise some ways of reducing prejudice between the white and black students. They devised the fascinating jigsaw technique.

Method: This involved dividing the class into small groups of racially mixed students, each of which had to work on a part of a lesson. The individuals in the groups first had to work together, and then communicated their group work to the rest of the class in order for the whole class to cover all of the material.

Results: When Aronson evaluated the strategy he found increased cooperation, self-esteem and academic performance. He also noted more positive perceptions of students in the other racial group, which would suggest that stereotypes were breaking down.

Conclusion: Aronson found that these new perceptions were not generalised to members of the racial group outside the class: these students saw each other as exceptions to the stereotypes, but the stereotypes themselves did not change very much, in fact.

So although cooperation strategies can reduce prejudice, the individual may not generalise these new attitudes to others when they are in a different setting. For example, they may learn in class to treat people of different cultures with respect, but this may not be considered when outside the classroom.

Creating empathy

Empathy is the ability to consider the emotions and feelings of another person. For example, if you see a student being bullied you may feel empathy for them and think that it must be horrible to be picked on like that; you are putting yourself in their shoes.

If we experience the effects of prejudice and discrimination, we might try to change our attitudes. Jane Elliott, a teacher at the time, wanted to test this idea with her class of nine-year-olds.

KEY STUDY

Elliott (1977)

Aim: To test the idea that if we experience prejudice and discrimination ourselves, it may help to reduce it in the future.

Method: Elliott divided the children in her class into two groups on the basis of their eye colour: blue-eyed and brown-eyed. Then she told them that brown-eyed people were better and more intelligent than those with blue eyes, so they would be given extra privileges. The blue-eyed students wore collars to distinguish them, and had to wait until the end of the line and have less break time.

The next day she told them she had made a mistake and that blue-eyed people were superior.

On the third day she told them the truth: that there were no such differences but that she wanted them to feel what it was like to be judged on the basis of one, irrelevant, physical feature which they could not change.

Results: The children started to behave according to these stereotypes: on day one the brown-eyed children became more dominant, produced better work and started to treat the blue-eyed children badly, while the blue-eyed children became angry or depressed and their work deteriorated. The next day the patterns of prejudice and discrimination quickly reversed.

Conclusion: This technique seemed to be effective in reducing prejudice. When Elliott contacted these students at 18 years of age, she found that they were more tolerant of differences between groups and more opposed to prejudice than a control group comprised of a class who had not gone through the brown-eyed/blue-eyed experience.

THE PRACTICAL APPLICATIONS OF REDUCING PREJUDICE

The likelihood that these techniques will reduce prejudice in everyday life will vary for several reasons. For example:

- The success of Elliott's work using empathy may have been due to the age of the children, whose stereotypes and attitudes were probably more flexible than those of adults. Creating empathy in adults with prejudiced views may be more difficult to accomplish
- The success of Aronson's jigsaw technique may have been due in part to the role of the teacher. The technique relies on the skill of

the teacher in establishing a norm of mutual respect and cooperation, treating each student equally regardless of race. The in-group was the class as a whole, but this does not reflect wider society. The social norms that support prejudice must also be tackled if efforts to reduce prejudice are to be generalised to a wider social context

- It may not always be possible to ensure that people who are prejudiced come into contact only with higher-status members of a discriminated group
- Even when these techniques fail in general terms, they may still be valuable in a restricted social setting, such as a school or workplace. However, these too are competitive environments, and it is this aspect that may provide a basis for hostility
- Even when prejudice is illegal, social norms may condone or even encourage it. A cross-cultural study carried out in Holland and America (Teun A. van Dijk, 1987) looked at how racism is communicated between white people. Results indicated that in the wider society it was not acceptable to show racism, but within various subgroups (such as the family, in the workplace, among neighbours), racist talk and behaviour were acceptable. We can conclude that making racism illegal may reduce but not eliminate it.

TEST YOURSELF

1 Define what is meant by the terms stereotyping, prejudice and discrimination.
2 State one example of a positive stereotype and one example of a negative stereotype.
3 Outline one difference between prejudice and discrimination.
4 What did Adorno say were the characteristics of a person with an authoritarian personality?
5 What is the difference between an 'in-group' and an 'out-group' according to Tajfel?
6 What happened in Sherif's Robbers Cave study?
7 How can prejudice be reduced? Outline one explanation.

CHAPTER 5

Research methods and ethics – part 1

WHAT YOU NEED TO KNOW FOR THE EXAMINATION

What you need to know for the examination:

Methods of investigation:
- The use of scientific methods and techniques that aim for objectivity
- The formulation of testable hypotheses
- Procedures for the experimental method of investigation: independent and dependent variables
- Advantages and disadvantages of this method of investigation (including ecological validity)

Methods of control, data analysis and data presentation:
- Experimental designs (independent groups, repeated measures and matched pairs) and advantages and disadvantages of each
- Target population, samples and sampling methods (random, opportunity, systematic and stratified)

and advantages and disadvantages of each
- The use of standardised procedures, identification and control of extraneous variables, instructions to participants
- Random allocation, counterbalancing and randomisation
- Calculations including mean, mode, median, range and percentages; anomalous results and their possible effects
- Graphical representations, including bar charts
- Research in natural and experimental settings, including advantages and limitations of each

Ethical considerations:
- A knowledge and understanding of the ethical issues in psychological research and ways of dealing with these issues

ASK YOURSELF

If somebody asked you to investigate human behaviour, how could you do it? Would you merely watch them? Would you interview them? Would you send them a survey in the post?

Once you have decided how to carry out the research, how will you analyse it? Would you do it numerically or in a written format?

There are many different ways that psychologists study behaviour. Each method (the way that it is carried out) includes a number of different issues that need to be considered when carrying out research in psychology.

Again, there are various ways that psychologists can present their findings and come to some sort of conclusion.

METHODS OF INVESTIGATION

Scientific method of investigation

The scientific method is gathering information, studying it to identify patterns or relationships, generating theories to explain these patterns and then devising a hypothesis in order to test the theory.

The method employed to test the hypothesis should be objective (fact based), standardised (the same throughout), replicable (can be repeated) and value free.

The closest the researcher can get to achieving these aims is to use a laboratory experiment, because of the high level of control. This means the researcher can attempt to control all of the variables within the investigation and allows them to test for cause and effect (one variable having an effect on another). A good example is the famous Stanley Milgram experiment (described in Chapter 7: Social influence, page 118). Milgram was able to control the investigation: he had fixed the roles of the teacher and learner, he had a confederate playing the role of the learner (the responses that supposedly came from the confederate were recorded on a tape, so that was standardised), and the person playing the role of the experimenter had a list of prods to use if the naive participant hesitated.

KEY TERM

Hypothesis – a precise and testable statement of what the researchers predict will be the outcome of the study.

Hypotheses

A **hypothesis** is a precise and testable statement of what the researcher predicts will be the outcome of the study.

In an **experiment** this is called the experimental hypothesis and an example would be: 'Participants sitting alone will respond faster to a call for help than participants sitting with two others.' This is a testable statement that the researchers can investigate.

So, the researchers have made a statement, the plan now is to test to see whether it holds true. They might do this by conducting a laboratory experiment (another good example of this is Bibb Latané and John Darley's research into bystander behaviour, described in Chapter 7: Social influence, pages 131–132).

ACTIVITY

You have been asked to conduct some psychological research and have been told what to investigate. Using the following aims (the purpose of an investigation) write a hypothesis for each one:

- To investigate whether boys have a better short-term memory than girls
- To investigate whether chocolate makes you happy.

Independent and dependent variables

Experiments enable researchers to test cause and effect. The researcher aims to keep all variables constant except the one they are investigating, which is the **independent variable**; this is the variable that is manipulated 'under the control of the experimenter', and then measures what effect this has on another variable, something else, called the **dependent variable**; this is the measured outcome. The dependent variable depends on the independent variable.

Unlike some other methods that researchers use, an experiment allows researchers to carefully change things and see what happens. The researcher doesn't need to rely on things changing all by themselves! They have great control over what happens.

Imagine you were interested in seeing whether it was really the case that staying up late ruined your ability to do school work. What you'd need to do, obviously, is stay up really late and then see if you had a really awful day's work in school the next day. Of course, it's not quite as simple as that. 'Late' can mean anything at all: 11pm, midnight or even 3am! 'Ability to do school work' can also mean anything at all: 'number of mistakes made in psychology', 'number of verbs in French remembered'. You, the researcher, need to decide what you are controlling and what you are measuring.

Let's say that 'ability to do school work' could really be something as simple as 'ability to remember things'. And 'late' can mean 10pm bedtime, 11pm bedtime or midnight bedtime. The thing you are *controlling* (the independent variable) is the time you went to bed. The thing you are *measuring* (the dependent variable) would be 'ability to remember things'.

KEY TERMS

Independent variable – the variable that is manipulated (controlled) by the experimenter.

Dependent variable – the measured outcome.

EXAM STYLE QUESTIONS

Identify the independent variable and the dependent variable from the following experiments:

1 An investigation was conducted into the effects of alcohol on reaction time.
2 An investigation was conducted into the number of hours' sleep and alertness the next day.

The example above is a straightforward way of measuring the dependent variable, but measuring behaviour is often more complex. In Elizabeth Loftus's famous study on eyewitness testimony (described in Chapter 1: Memory, pages 20–21), she wanted to investigate the effect of leading questions on a person's memory. Participants were shown a video clip of a car crash and then asked the question: 'How fast were the cars going when they hit/smashed the other car?' She split the participants into different groups and each group was asked the same question but with either the verb 'hit' or 'smashed'. The two verbs were the independent variable in her experiment, and the estimate of the speed of the car was the dependent variable.

In an experimental condition, it is really important that it is only the independent variable that affects the dependent variable.

Experimental methods of investigation

Each method of investigation has a general type of procedure, as described below. When psychologists plan research, they choose the method that is most appropriate to what they are investigating. Here we will consider the three different types of procedure that belong to the experimental method: laboratory, field and natural experiments.

Laboratory experiments

In a laboratory experiment there is a high level of control because researchers can isolate cause and effect by controlling other variables. The psychologist decides where the experiment will take place, at what time, with which participants, in what circumstances and using a standardised procedure.

There are lots of examples of laboratory experiments throughout the book – look out for the Research Methods links.

Advantages and disadvantages of laboratory experiments

Advantages	Disadvantages
• It is easy to replicate a laboratory experiment (to repeat it using the same procedures). This is easily done because the researcher has control over the variables. • An experiment can gather quantitative data (numerical data), which can be easily analysed.	• The artificiality of the setting can intimidate participants or make them more obedient. This in turn may produce unnatural behaviour and results that do not generalise to real life. • Demand characteristics: these are any features of the research that may affect participants' behaviour, making them act unnaturally or look for cues to tell them what the research is about and behave accordingly. Being in a strange setting, and being treated in a rather formal, impersonal way by researchers, remind participants that something artificial is going on. One way of reducing demand characteristics in the laboratory is to conduct the experiment without the participants realising it. • The artificial nature of the laboratory setting raises the question of ecological validity. Because results are generated from a situation that is unlike everyday life, to what extent can the conclusions be generalised to everyday life?

Field experiments

In a field experiment the psychologist manipulates the independent variable but the experiment takes place in a real-life setting, for example in a university (for example Latané and Darley's into bystander behaviour, Chapter 7: Social influence, page 133) or on the New York subway (Irving Piliavin's study into 'Good Samaritanism', Chapter 7: Social influence, page 135).

KEY TERMS

Demand characteristics – any features of the research that may affect participants' behaviour, making them act unnaturally or look for cues to tell them what the research is about and behave accordingly.

Ecological validity – the degree to which the findings from a study can be generalised beyond the research setting.

Advantages and disadvantages of field experiments

Advantages	Disadvantages
• Because the study is taking place in a natural setting, the behaviour is more likely to be more natural compared with a laboratory experiment; there is higher ecological validity. • There is less chance of demand characteristics –with the majority of field experiments the participants do not know that they are taking part in an investigation.	• Deception – because participants do not know that they are taking part in an investigation in the majority of field experiments, the researchers are deceiving them. However, deception is often necessary. • As the participants are being deceived, the researchers do not have their consent, let alone full, informed consent. However, this cannot always be obtained (as demand characteristics would then be present, and real behaviour would not be demonstrated).

Quasi or natural experiments

The quasi or natural experiment is one in which the independent variable occurs in real life, so the researcher cannot 'create' a difference for the purpose of the experiment.

In a quasi experiment the independent variable may be age, gender or race. In a natural experiment the independent variable is already occurring.

An example is the research that was done to test the effects of the media on eating disorders. On a Caribbean island where televisions had not been introduced, researchers found that there were no diagnoses of anorexia nervosa. However, a few years later when televisions had been introduced to the island, a number of girls had been diagnosed with it (Anne Becker *et al.*, 2002). This is an example of a natural experiment, as the behaviour occurred naturally. The researchers did not manipulate anything.

Some ideas that could be investigated using a natural experiment are:

• The introduction of the smoking ban in the UK – has this affected sales of cigarettes, or the number of people dying from smoking-related illnesses?
• How people cope in a hurricane.

None of these factors can be controlled: they occur/have occurred naturally.

Advantages and disadvantages of natural experiments

Advantages	Disadvantages
• Natural experiments allow researchers to investigate behaviour that, for ethical reasons, could not be studied or created. • Because participants are unaware that they are taking part in an investigation, there will be less chance of demand characteristics and more natural behaviour.	• Because the independent variable is not controlled by the investigator, there is less control from the researcher's point of view.

METHODS OF CONTROL, DATA ANALYSIS AND DATA PRESENTATION

Experimental design

In an experiment, researchers might want to know if one group of people are better at something than another group of people. They would run their experiment and collect a lot of numerical data. One set of numbers would be from one group and another set from another group. In this type of experiment we have two separate groups.

In an investigation to see if caffeine (found in coffee and tea) affects a person's ability to play a computer game, we could have two separate groups: one that would drink coffee before they undertake the task, and the other not drinking coffee before the task. From this we could determine which one was better.

Sometimes one group experiences the independent variable (called the experimental group) and the other group does not (this is the control group). The way in which participants are assigned to groups is called the experimental design. The three types of experimental design are described below.

Independent-groups design

Here there are different participants in each group. Each group is independent of the other. In laboratory and some field experiments

KEY TERMS

Experimental group – the group that experiences the independent variable.

Control group – the group that does not experience the independent variable.

KEY TERM

Random allocation – randomly assigning participants into different groups.

the researcher is able to choose which participants are assigned to the experimental group and which to the control group.

So, for example, we could test the effect of different music on a person's recall. The experimental group could be split into two: one group could listen to pop music, and the other group to classical music. Both groups are given the same memory test to do. The control group would complete the memory test but no music would be played.

Assigning participants to groups should be done by random allocation; this ensures that each participant has an equal chance of being assigned to one group or the other.

Strengths and weaknesses of the independent-groups design

Strengths	Weaknesses
• It is the quickest and easiest way of allocating participants; because they are assigned randomly to groups there are no order effects (which occur with repeated measures: see below).	• People vary in their experiences, attitudes, intelligence, alertness, moods – these are participant variables. Because participants are assigned randomly, the researchers do not know, for example, whether one group comprises most of the more alert or skilled participants. If this were the case, these participant variables might produce differences between the results from the two groups that are not due to the independent variable. A large sample is needed to reduce this effect.

Repeated-measures design

Here every participant goes through both experiences (the experimental condition and the control condition). So, for example, the participants taking part in the music and memory experiment would experience all three conditions: pop music, classical music and no music.

Strengths and weaknesses of the repeated-measures design

Strengths	Weaknesses
• Because the same people are in both conditions, there are no participant variables. • Requires fewer participants, as the participants are in both conditions.	• There are drawbacks to this design that might produce biased results. For instance, the participant may guess the aim of the study when they take part in the second condition, so demand characteristics may affect the results. • Taking part in both conditions may produce order effects, or practice effects as they are sometimes known, which may affect participants' performance.

To combat the influence of order effects or demand characteristics on the results, **counterbalancing** should be carried out: this means reversing the order of the conditions for the participants.

The sample is split into two; one half does the experimental condition (A), then the control condition (B); the other half does the control condition (B), then the experimental condition (A). This is called the ABBA design. Although order effects still occur for each participant, because they occur equally in both groups they balance each other out in the results.

The example of investigation into music and memory could be counterbalanced by having half of the group do the no music condition and then the pop/classical music condition, and the other half doing the pop/classical music condition and then the no music condition.

Matched-pairs design

This type of design involves matching participants in pairs on the basis of variables relevant to the study, such as age, gender, intelligence, reading ability or socioeconomic background. This may require pre-tests in order to ensure good matching, and then one of each pair is randomly assigned to the experimental condition and the other to the control condition. The perfect matched-pairs design is one that uses identical twins, assigning one to each condition.

KEY TERMS

Order effects – experiencing both the experimental and control conditions in a repeated-measures design may affect participants' performance by either damaging it (because they have become bored or tired of repeating the task) or improving it (because they have already done a similar task: the practice effect).

Counterbalancing – reversing the order of the conditions for half of the participants.

Strengths and weaknesses of the matched-pairs design

Strengths	Weaknesses
• Because participants experience only one condition of the experiment there are no order effects (so counterbalancing is not necessary).	• This method can be more expensive and time consuming than the others. • Some participant variables may still affect the results.

EXAM STYLE QUESTIONS

Read the following information and decide which type of experimental design it is:

1 Researcher A wanted to investigate whether intelligence is genetic. He used 40 identical twins in his sample and gave both twins an IQ test.

2 Researcher B wanted to investigate whether age had anything to do with driving ability. Pensioners were assigned to one group and new drivers were assigned to another group; they both took part in a driving-simulation task.

3 Researcher C wanted to investigate if the type of chocolate eaten improves the mood of a person. Condition A involved participants eating a very expensive box of chocolates; condition B involved participants eating a cheaper version of the box of chocolates. Participants were then required to fill in a questionnaire to rate their mood. Participants experienced both conditions.

Target populations, samples and sampling methods

The participants in research – the sample – should be as representative as possible of the target population. This target population may be six-year-olds, male adults, parents, insecurely attached children or witnesses of crime. The more representative the sample, the more confident the researcher can be that the results can be generalised to the target population. Having said this, very few samples in research are truly representative, as you will see from the following descriptions of sampling methods (ways of choosing participants).

Random sampling

Be warned, this is not what you think it is! Random sampling is actually quite controlled. It means that every member of the target population has an equal chance of being selected. For instance, in a study with a target population of local seven-year-olds, the names of every seven-year-old from all the local primary schools are gathered.

Each child must have an equal chance of being selected, so the names of all the children might be written on a slip of paper, put in a box or bag and mixed up. To select 20 participants, 20 names would be taken out of the box. Another way to do it might be for each child to be given a number and the sample selected using the above method, or a computer might select random numbers.

ACTIVITY

How could you gather a random sample of people living in your area? How could you obtain the information, and how would you try and make sure the sample was really random?

Strengths and weaknesses of random sampling

Strengths	Weaknesses
• Random sampling is the best technique for providing an unbiased, representative sample of a target population.	• It can be very time consuming and is often impossible to carry out, particularly when you have a large target population.

Opportunity sampling

Researchers rarely use random sampling; they have to rely on participants who are more easily accessible. For example, a psychologist wishing to study pre-school children might use the children who are attending the university crèche and who fit the criteria for age, sex and so on. This is an example of opportunity sampling: anyone who is available, and agrees to take part in research, can become a participant. Hence, the researcher takes the opportunity to use them in the research.

Opportunity sampling occurs in field experiments. For example, if we wanted to test helping behaviour, the best way to do so would be to conduct research in a real-life setting. So, we could have a confederate on a bus, get him/her to fall over and then see if people help and time how long they take to help. The sample of participants would be the passengers on the bus.

Strengths and weaknesses of opportunity sampling

Strengths	Weaknesses
• It is quick and cheap in comparison with other methods.	• As it only uses people who are available at the time, the sample may not be representative of society in general.

Systematic sampling

This means selecting participants at fixed intervals from the target population. This could be every third person on a class register or every sixth person who comes out of a shop. Although each person does not stand an equal chance of being selected (as in random sampling) at least there is no opportunity for bias (in favour of one side/group) in selecting participants, for example because they look helpful or the child is fairly well behaved.

It's important that the potential participants are as randomised as possible. If you were choosing participants from a list of pupils in a school arranged by class (years 1, 2, 3...), you might end up picking all first years. This problem is called periodicity; in this example it would be avoided by mixing all the names up first.

Strengths and weaknesses of systematic sampling

Strengths	Weaknesses
• Fairly cheap and fast. • Eliminates the possibility of bias in selecting participants.	• Researchers need to ensure that the list does not contain a hidden order (periodicity).

Stratified sampling

A stratified sample provides a sample that is in proportion, in the relevant characteristics, to the target population. Imagine you are conducting a survey of women to ask questions about their attitude to childcare. You consider that the relevant characteristics are the types of work women do, so you need to find what proportion of females in the whole population are self-employed, professional, manual workers, unemployed and so on. This information is available from census data (a census is collected by the government every few years from households and information is given as to who lives where, their occupations, number of children etc.). These categories must be represented in the same proportions in your sample. If 10 per cent of females are self-employed, then in a sample of 50, five should be self-employed. To get the required numbers in each category, participants should be random-sampled from the target population.

Strengths and weaknesses of stratified sampling

Strengths	Weaknesses
• Provides a very representative sample.	• Time consuming and expensive.

EXAM STYLE QUESTIONS

Identify the sampling methods used in the following investigations:

1 Researcher A wanted a sample of gym members and so put all their membership details into a hat and picked out ten to take part in his investigation.
2 Researcher B wanted a sample of sixth-form students. She chose every tenth person off the school roll.
3 Researcher C wanted a sample of people who use public transport. He waited at a local bus stop and asked people who were waiting to catch a bus.

Standard procedures, controlling variables and instructions to participants

To be confident that the independent variable caused the dependent variable, the researcher must try to control all other aspects (or variables) in the experiment. Here we consider ways in which the researcher can increase control over the research environment, and so have greater confidence in the results that emerge (in other words, that the independent variable has definitely caused the dependent variable).

Standardised procedures

To ensure that all participants have the same experience, researchers should ensure that they are all tested:

- In the same place, with the same equipment and materials placed in the same way
- Under the same conditions, so the level of lighting, noise and heat remains the same for all participants
- At roughly the same time of day, as people may behave differently if tested at nine o'clock in the morning rather than five o'clock at night.

Controlling variables

If variables are not controlled, they may influence the results and so make them invalid. Consider a memory task comparing recall of words that are organised by meaning with recall of words presented randomly. If the participants in the 'organised' group saw the words but the participants in the random group heard them read out, then it could be the difference in the way that the words were presented that created any difference in recall, rather than whether the words were organised or random. This difference in the way the words were presented is called a **confounding variable**.

Figure 5.1 Is it faster to catch the bus home or to cycle? The confounding variable might be the fitness level of the cyclist: a really fit person may beat the bus home but an unfit cyclist would not. It's nothing to do with the ease with which the bike slips between the traffic; it's to do with how fit the cyclist is!

Another confounding variable in this example might be that memory in a task *could* be influenced by how awake students were. Those tested early in the morning may well be sleepier than those tested at 1pm.

In order to control variables, all participants must undergo the same experience, except for the independent variable. A standardised procedure, with standardised instructions, must be devised and followed for each participant.

Standardised instructions

Participants should be given identical instructions in exactly the same way. This is particularly important if the research requires them to perform a task. Sometimes the instructions are written down and participants are asked to read them. This eliminates any possible bias that may creep in if they were spoken, but some participants may have difficulty reading or understanding the instructions. For this reason any instructions must be simple, clear and unambiguous.

Calculations

Once all of the above has been considered and the investigation has been conducted, we need to look at the data that have been collected. In this section we will consider quantitative data (data that can be analysed in a numerical sense).

There are various calculations that can be used to analyse data and provide some sort of meaning to the end result of an investigation. These include the mean, median, mode, range and percentages. We will consider each one in turn.

The mean

The **mean** (often referred to as the average) is calculated by adding up all of the scores in a condition and dividing it by the number of participants that there were in that condition. So, if you had 20 people, each standing on one leg for as long as they could, you would add up all their 'standing-on-one-leg' times and divide by 20 to get the mean 'standing-on-one-leg' time.

The mean makes use all of the scores. However, if there are scores in the data that are extreme (known as **anomalous**) these can distort the mean and so not give an accurate representation.

For example, in the activity above there is a score of 0 in condition B. This could be regarded as an anomalous score as it will distort the mean.

ACTIVITY

Imagine you had investigated the effects of music on a person's short-term memory. There were two conditions: condition A included participants listening to classical music while being shown 15 items, and condition B included participants listening to rock music while being shown the same 15 items. Each condition included 10 participants. Have a look at the data collection sheet below:

Condition A	Condition B
12	6
11	8
9	6
11	6
9	7
9	9
11	0
8	8
9	9
10	9

What are the mean scores for condition A and condition B?

The median

The **median** is calculated by looking at the middle score in a set of data; to do this you first need to place the score in value order.

For an odd number of figures, the median is simply the middle number (the one with an equal number of scores higher and lower than it).

ACTIVITY

Work out the median from this set of data:

5, 7, 3, 3, 8, 2, 9

If there is an even number of scores, you have to take the two central values and work out their mean (average) – simply add them up and divide them by two. So, for example, if we had the data:

4, 5, 3, 3, 7, 8, 6, 3

First place in value order:

3, 3, 3, **4**, **5**, 6, 7, 8

The two central values are 4 and 5, so the median is (4 + 5) / 2 = 4.5.

The mode

The **mode** (French for fashion) is the most frequently occurring score (that is, the most fashionable score!). So, if we wanted to work out the most frequently occurring score in a maths test, we would calculate the mode. Let's have a look at this set of data:

5, 7, 3, 3, 3, 8, 2, 9

The mode here is 3.

Range

The **range** is a measure of dispersion, that is, the difference between the highest and lowest score in a condition. If we were to calculate the range of the following set of data:

17, 3, 11, 19, 7, 9

We would subtract the lowest score (3) from the highest score (19), giving us an answer of 16.

Percentages

If we wanted to work out the **percentage** for each student in a psychology test, we would divide the score that they achieved on the test by the total maximum score and then multiply the answer by 100 (per cent means per hundred).

For example, if Reg has achieved 45 marks out of a possible 60:

45 / 60 = 0.75
0.75 × 100 = 75%

ACTIVITY

Have a go at working out the percentages for these test scores:

Candidate	Score achieved on the test	Maximum score possible
Dawn	73	90
Louise	27	50
Lizzy	15	65

Graphical representations

Once the data has been calculated, it is often useful to present it in a graph: this can make the information easier for people to interpret and understand.

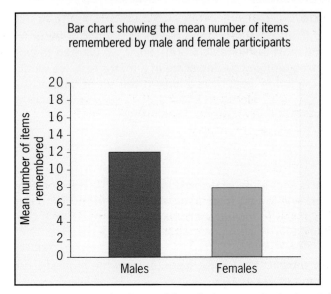

Figure 5.2 The categories (males and females) are on the horizontal axis and the frequency (how many items they remembered) is shown on the vertical axis

Bar charts

A **bar chart** is one way to display data in categories.

The categories can be shown along the horizontal axis and the frequencies (how often something occurs) can be shown along the vertical axis. The bars (or rectangles) should not touch each other: keep them separate! Ideally the bars should be arranged in ascending or descending order. Both of the axes should be clearly labelled, and an appropriate title should be given.

ETHICAL CONSIDERATIONS

Ethics are the desirable standards of behaviour we use towards others. If we behave ethically, then we treat others with respect and have concern for their well-being. Psychologists have legal and moral responsibilities to those who help them in their research: every individual has rights and these must be respected and protected. Ethical concerns apply to animals as well, but our concern here is for humans.

Participants in research put their trust in the researchers. If these researchers betray the participants' trust this discredits the profession and makes it less likely that others will agree to take part in research in the future.

The British Psychological Society (BPS) has published guidelines specifying ethical concerns and how they must be addressed. These guidelines apply to anyone working within psychology, so this includes students of psychology. Some of the most important ethical concerns are described below.

The invasion of personal privacy

The privacy of participants must be protected. This includes confidentiality, observations and the right to withdrawal if participants feel uncomfortable.

Confidentiality

Participants, and the data gained from them, must be kept anonymous unless they give their full consent. It must not be possible to identify participants from any reporting of the research, such as in an academic journal or a newspaper article.

Observations

If participants are observed in public, in circumstances where anyone could observe them, privacy is not an issue. Having said this, if the observer is obvious to those being watched, perhaps taking notes, this may cause discomfort or distress, which is not acceptable. However, when observers are hidden, then privacy is violated and this contravenes the BPS guidelines.

Withdrawal

When participants agree to take part in research they do not know the extent to which you will encroach upon their feelings, emotions or sense of what is appropriate. This is why researchers must gain informed consent (see below) and also tell participants that they can withdraw at any time during the research if they wish to do so.

Participants should also be reminded of their right to withdraw if it is a long study or if they appear to be distressed. By reminding them of the right to withdraw you are stressing that they are under no obligation to continue and can act to protect themselves at any time if they feel uncomfortable.

If participants initially agree and then decide to withdraw that agreement at the end of the study or after they have been debriefed, all data and information about them must be deleted from the research.

Minimising distress and deception

Distress

Researchers must ensure that those taking part in research will not be caused distress. They must be protected from physical and mental harm. This means that you must not embarrass, upset, frighten, offend or harm participants. For example, if your study involved showing participants gruesome pictures, this could upset them.

This is also an issue in cross-cultural research, where a question asked may offend the norms of one culture but not another.

Deception

Deception is sometimes necessary in order to avoid demand characteristics affecting the results, but participants must be deceived as little as possible, and any deception must not cause distress. If you have gained participants' informed consent by deception, then they will have agreed to take part without knowing what they were consenting to.

The true nature of the research should be revealed at the earliest possible opportunity, or at least during debriefing. If the participant is likely to object or be distressed once they discover the true nature of the research at debriefing, then the study is unacceptable.

If serious deception has been involved, the researcher must ensure that the participant understands why and feels comfortable about their part in the research.

Informed consent and debriefing

Informed consent

Before the study begins, the researcher must outline to the participant what the research entails, and then ask if they consent to take part. If the participants are children, someone who is responsible for them (a parent or guardian) must be told what is involved, and they must give consent. Having gained this, the researcher must still ask the child if they are willing to take part, and the child must agree.

However, it is not always possible to gain informed consent. This is acceptable as long as what happens to the participants is something that could just as easily happen to them in everyday life. For example, if your research involves observing people in a bus queue, those people may be observed by anyone when they are in the queue, so informed consent is not essential.

Debriefing

Participants must be thoroughly debriefed at the end of the study. They must be given a general idea of what the researcher was investigating and why, and their part in the research should be explained. They must be assured that their results are confidential. They must be told if they have been deceived and it must be justified to them. They must be asked if they have any questions and these should be answered honestly and as fully as possible.

Participants may have experienced distress through their experience, perhaps when they hear they have been deceived or if the procedure caused them anxiety, embarrassment or loss of self-esteem. It is the researcher's responsibility to check on the participants' physical and psychological well-being as part of the debriefing process. If necessary, they should be followed up to ensure there are no ill-effects later on.

Summary

It is sometimes difficult to plan research within these guidelines. Most research requires some degree of deception, for example. Nevertheless, many psychologists have devised clever ways of running studies that are within these guidelines; others have not. You can see that some of the research reported in this book contravenes these guidelines, possibly because the research took place before the guidelines became so strict.

EXAM STYLE QUESTIONS

A psychologist conducted an experiment to see if there was a gender difference in spelling ability. Two groups were used (condition A and condition B): condition A consisted of 20 females all aged ten, condition B consisted of 20 males all aged ten.

They had been sat in the school canteen when the psychologist approached them and asked them if they wanted to take part. Both conditions were given exactly the same list of words to spell (ten words in total). The experimenter read out the list of words to both groups (both the males and females were in the room at the same time). The students had to spell the word that they were asked to on a piece of paper. The pieces of paper were collected in at the end of the experiment and analysed for the results. The students did not know the true purpose of the investigation.

1 Write a suitable hypothesis for this experiment.
2 Identify the independent variable.
3 Identify the dependent variable.
4 Identify the experimental design used in this experiment.
5 Identify the sampling method used here.
6 What would be the most appropriate way to analyse the results in a numerical sense?
7 Identify one ethical issue the psychologist should have considered before conducting the experiment.
8 Outline one way in which the psychologist could have dealt with the ethical issue you have identified in question 7.

UNDERSTANDING OTHER PEOPLE

6 Learning

WHAT YOU NEED TO KNOW FOR THE EXAMINATION

What you need to know for the examination:

- Principles of classical conditioning – unconditioned stimulus, unconditioned response, conditioned stimulus, conditioned response, extinction, spontaneous recovery, generalisation, discrimination, the contributions of Pavlov
- Principles of operant conditioning – Thorndike's law of effect and the contributions of Skinner. Behaviour shaping; the distinction between positive reinforcement, negative reinforcement and punishment
- Applications – descriptions and evaluation of attempts to apply conditioning procedures to the treatment of phobias (including flooding and systematic desensitisation) and to change unwanted behaviour (including aversion therapy and token economy). The ethical implications of such attempts.

ACTIVITY

Imagine you are writing a psychology dictionary for GCSE students. Write the dictionary definition for the word 'learning'.

Most psychologists agree that learning is a relatively permanent change in behaviour that is due to some experience, for example learning how to talk, how to dress ourselves, ride a bike etc.

Learning is essential for all human beings and without a learning process we just wouldn't be able to function. Many different psychologists have attempted to explain what learning is and how it occurs, and as a result a number of different theories have been put forward. In this chapter, we will focus on the theory that suggests that we learn through conditioning. There are two types of conditioning: classical conditioning and operant conditioning.

KEY TERM

Learning – a relatively permanent change in behaviour that is due to some experience.

ASK YOURSELF

Why do you think the dogs started to salivate when they heard the footsteps?

EXAM STYLE QUESTIONS

Outline what is meant by the term 'learning'.

CLASSICAL CONDITIONING

Classical conditioning was discovered by a Russian scientist, Ivan Pavlov, in the early 1900s. He noticed that when dogs in his laboratory heard the footsteps of the researcher they started to salivate (an automatic – or reflex – response that occurs when an animal smells food).

Figure 6.1 Pavlov's dog

Pavlov came to the conclusion that the dogs were associating the footsteps with the food, because the two things (the stimuli) had occurred together so many times.

ACTIVITY

Carry out a mini observation on your pets (if you don't have any, ask your friends and family if any of their pets do similar things). Do any of your pets do this?

- My cat starts to purr when he hears the electric tin opener because he thinks that he is going to get some tuna.
- If I pick up my dog's lead, he runs to the front door because he thinks he is going for a walk.

Record what your pets do and explain this behaviour in relation to classical conditioning.

Normally the stimulus of an electric tin opener wouldn't cause a cat to purr; the food in the tin would. And a lead wouldn't cause a dog to run to the front door; the fact that he is going for a walk would.

In order to understand how Pavlov's dogs had *learned* this association, he set up an experiment.

KEY STUDY

Pavlov's dogs

Aim: Pavlov was studying digestion in dogs – he wasn't originally intending to study conditioning.

Method: He presented food in a bowl to a dog several times and, in the end, the dog salivated even when the bowl was empty. Pavlov had conditioned it to salivate to an empty bowl. Pavlov then decided to further his research by giving the dogs food at the same time as ringing a bell (a neutral stimulus).

Results: After several times, the dogs salivated (a response) to the bell.

Conclusion: The dogs associated the bell with salivation. Normally, footsteps and a bell would not cause a dog to salivate, would they? But the dogs learned to associate the footsteps and the bell with the food and, hence, they salivated when these stimuli were present.

RESEARCH METHODS

Pavlov's study is an example of a laboratory experiment. A description of a laboratory experiment and its strengths and weaknesses can be found in Chapter 5: Research methods and ethics – part 1, pages 70–71.

The reflex response (the salivation) is called the unconditional response. The stimulus that causes the salivation (food) is called the unconditional stimulus. The bell is called the conditional stimulus and when the salivation has become associated with the bell, it becomes the conditional response.

KEY TERMS

Unconditional response (UCR) – Behaviour over which one has no control; behaviour that is automatic.

Unconditional stimulus (UCS) – Anything that causes an unconditioned response.

Conditional stimulus (CS) – The stimulus that is presented with the unconditioned stimulus.

Conditional response (CR) – The response that occurs when the conditioned stimulus is presented.

Neutral stimulus (NS) – a stimulus that initially produces no specific response other than to focus attention; in classical conditioning when used together with an unconditioned stimulus, the neutral stimulus becomes a conditioned stimulus.

EXAM STYLE QUESTIONS

Identify the unconditional stimulus, the unconditional response, the neutral stimulus, the conditional stimulus and the conditional response from the following example:

Ben, who is six years old, went to the dentist to have a tooth filled. The female dentist wore a white coat. The filling was quite painful and now every time Ben sees anyone wearing a white coat, he panics.

Key concepts based on the principles of classical conditioning

Key concept	Explanation
Extinction	If the conditioned stimulus (the bell) is repeatedly presented without the unconditioned stimulus (food), the conditioned response (salivation) gradually decreases.
Spontaneous recovery	Pavlov found that if, after a delay, the animal was presented with the conditioned stimulus (the bell) again, the conditioned response (salivation) often reappeared.
Generalisation	This occurs when the response is triggered by a similar stimulus to the original one.
Discrimination	Pavlov noticed that if the dog was given food only when the same bell was sounded, after several trials they only salivated to the original bell, not to any other bells.

The research that Pavlov did with the dogs is a very famous study and the ideas behind it have been used by many other psychologists in their research.

KEY STUDY

Watson and Raynor (1920): Little Albert

Aim: To see if it was possible to condition somebody to become phobic using the principles of classical conditioning.

KEY STUDY – (continued)

Method: Little Albert, an 11-month-old baby, was brought to the laboratory of John Watson and Rosalie Rayner. He was happily playing with a white rat (a real one!) when a metal bar was struck close to him to make a loud noise. This caused him to jump and develop a fear response. This was done several times while he played with the rat.

Results: The researcher then stopped striking the metal bar and gave Albert the rat to play with. He was still very frightened and tried to crawl away.

Conclusion: Albert had learned to associate the rat with a fear response. Through classical conditioning he had learned to show a fear response towards an object that he had not previously feared. Although he was conditioned to fear only white rats, this fear generalised to a white rabbit and other white objects.

Figure 6.2 Little Albert was the subject of a famous experiment into classical conditioning

EXAM STYLE QUESTIONS

Describe and evaluate one study in which classical conditioning was investigated. Include in your answer the method used in the study, the results obtained, the conclusion drawn and an evaluation of the study.

ASK YOURSELF

Why was Albert so afraid of the rat?

ACTIVITY

What are the ethical issues associated with this study?

RESEARCH METHODS

Watson and Raynor's study is an example of a laboratory experiment. A description of a laboratory experiment and its strengths and weaknesses can be found in Chapter 5: Research methods and ethics – part 1, pages 70–71.

Little Albert's behaviour can be explained through the process of classical conditioning. This process is shown in the table below, using the key terminology mentioned before.

	Stimulus	Response
The situation before the condition starts	White rat Loud noise (UCS)	No response Fear response (UCR)
During trials	White rat and loud noise	Fear response
When condition has occurred	White rat (CS)	Fear response (CR)

To reinforce your learning, below is a table with the key concepts that you learnt about before, but with examples relating to this famous research.

EXAM STYLE QUESTIONS

Using the key concept and the research example, provide an explanation for the following terms:

Key concept	Example	Explanation
Extinction	Little Albert's fear of the rat could have been unlearned (although Watson and Raynor did not do this). For example, he would be given the rat to play with but there would be no loud noise. Eventually he would no longer associate the noise with the rat and his fear would be extinguished.	
Spontaneous recovery	Although Little Albert's fear behaviour may have become extinct, it would not be forgotten.	
Generalisation	Little Albert's fear became generalised to a white rabbit and cotton wool. Pavlov also noticed that if he rang bells with different pitches, the dogs still salivated.	
Discrimination	Pavlov noticed that if the dogs were given food only when the same bell is sounded, after several trials, they only salivated to the original bell, not to any other bells.	

EXAM STYLE QUESTIONS

Read the scenario below and tick the correct box to say which one is the correct answer:

David has a puppy called Harvey. For the last few weeks he has given Harvey a biscuit from the kitchen cupboard below the sink as a treat. Harvey knows where the treats are kept. When David opens the cupboard to get some washing-up liquid out, Harvey thinks that he is getting a treat and wags his tail.

	Unconditioned response	Unconditioned stimulus	Conditioned stimulus	Conditioned response
Harvey wags his tail when he eats a biscuit given to him as a treat by David				
David opens the cupboard to get some washing-up liquid out and Harvey wags his tail.				

ASK YOURSELF

Imagine you have just completed a piece of psychology homework and achieved a grade A for it. Your teacher praises you ('well done') and gives you a bar of chocolate as a reward. What should happen next time you get a piece of psychology homework to do?

Classical conditioning has been used to explain a number of different behaviours.

ACTIVITY

Write down three examples of how classical conditioning can be applied in everyday situations.

OPERANT CONDITIONING

In theory, you should repeat the behaviour as you would like to think that, if you did well again, you would get the same reward. This is the basis of the second theory that attempts to explain learning, which belongs to the Behaviourist approach. It is known as operant conditioning. It is still concerned with learning but focuses on the consequences of the behaviour influencing whether or not the behaviour will be repeated.

Thorndike's law of effect

Edward Thorndike (1898) was conducting research with cats at a similar time to when Pavlov was experimenting with his dogs.

KEY STUDY

Thorndike (1898)

Aim: To investigate the effect of consequences on learned behaviour in animals.

Method: He noticed that a hungry cat could learn to open a latch so that it could escape its cage and eat some fish that was outside. Early on in the trial, the cat accidentally knocked the latch as it was turning around in the cage trying to get to the fish. Each time the cat was returned to the cage.

Results: Each time the cat returned to the cage, there was less time before it opened the latch and escaped again.

Conclusion: The cat had learnt to associate pressing the lever with getting food (a pleasant consequence).

As a result of these experiments, Thorndike put forward a theory called 'the law of effect'. In this he stated that behaviour that leads to pleasant circumstances (in this case, eating the fish) will be learnt and repeated. On the other hand, behaviour that leads to unpleasant circumstances will still be learnt but not be repeated.

Thorndike suggested that the consequences must occur soon after the behaviour is performed if learning is to occur. This is because the association is formed between the behaviour (lever pressing) and the pleasant consequences (food).

EXAM STYLE QUESTIONS

Describe and evaluate one study in which classical conditioning was investigated. Include in your answer the method used in the study, the results obtained, the conclusion drawn and an evaluation of the study.

Skinner's theory

Burrhus Frederic Skinner (1938) was interested in Thorndike's work and decided to test his ideas further. He developed a 'Skinner box', which involved an animal inside and a lever or key that could deliver

KEY TERMS

Positive reinforcement – leads to behaviour that is repeated because the consequences have been positive and the individual finds it rewarding.

Negative reinforcement – takes place when our behaviour stops something nasty happening. For example, a child cries while out shopping, so the parent gives the child a sweet and the child stops crying. Next time the child cries the parent is likely to repeat the sweet-giving behaviour because, for the parent, giving the sweet stopped something nasty (the child crying) happening.

Punishment – a consequence that weakens behaviour (makes it less likely to happen).

a food pellet. As Thorndike found, the animal became quicker and quicker at pressing the lever because they knew to expect a pleasant consequence (food).

Skinner noticed that once the animal had realised that the lever produced food, they continued to press the lever, and hence the behaviour was repeated. Skinner concluded from his research that behaviour can be shaped and maintained by its consequences.

ACTIVITY

Go to the British Psychological Society website and find the *Guidelines for psychologists who work with animals*. Make notes on how psychologists should care for animals. What should they do and what should they not do?

A problem with using animals in research is that we can't normally generalise from cats/rats to humans. However, Skinner developed a number of different principles that he claimed were also applicable to humans.

Skinner claimed that both humans and animals will use the consequences of behaviour to shape future behaviour. He called this reinforcement. There are two types: positive reinforcement and negative reinforcement.

Some examples of when you might use positive reinforcement in school/college:

- Your teacher praises you in front of the class for an excellent piece of homework
- Your friends comment on your outfit, so you wear it again.

Punishment should make a behaviour less likely to happen. For example, a child is running around in the supermarket and knocking into people. The parent shouts at the child. The child stops running around and calms down. The shouting has acted as a punishment.

Skinner suggested that punishment doesn't always work as it doesn't show what the undesirable behaviour should be replaced with. For example, if the parent were to explain or show the child how to behave in a supermarket and not run around the store disrupting things, the punishment is more likely to be effective.

A summary of operant conditioning

Principle	Effect on behaviour	Consequence
Positive reinforcement	Strengthens	Pleasant
Negative reinforcement	Strengthens	Stops something unpleasant
Punishment	Weakens	Unpleasant

Behaviour shaping is another concept that belongs to operant conditioning. Reinforcement can be used to create completely new behaviour by shaping random behaviour and building up a sequence of behaviours.

Skinner demonstrated this by teaching pigeons to play ping pong. He provided reinforcement every time a pigeon showed behaviour that was close to what he wanted, such as providing food when a pigeon moved towards the ball. Once that behaviour was established, reinforcement was withdrawn and provided only when the animal touched the ball. By reinforcing a narrower range of behaviours, the pigeon would eventually go to the ball and hit it with its beak.

EXAM STYLE QUESTIONS

Read the scenarios below and identify whether they are positive reinforcers, negative reinforcers or punishers:

1 Melanie gets a glowing year-13 report from her subject teachers. Her parents take her to a theme park.
2 Helen has been sent home from school for unruly behaviour. She has been grounded for a week and had her pocket money stopped.
3 Danielle's mum won't allow her to stay up late to watch TV as it is past her bedtime. She cries and sulks. Her mum gives in and lets her watch TV.

TEST YOURSELF

1 How do psychologists define learning?
2 In Pavlov's experiments with dogs, what was the unconditioned stimulus?
3 What did Pavlov condition his dogs to do?
4 Write a sentence describing how Little Albert learned to fear the white rat.
5 Explain how the Little Albert experiment demonstrates classical conditioning.
6 According to Thorndike, what happens when behaviour has pleasant consequences?
7 Draw a picture of a rat in a Skinner box and explain how the rat demonstrates learned behaviour.
8 Complete these sentences:
   • Positive reinforcement occurs when ...
   • Negative reinforcement occurs when ...
   • When behaviour is punished it is less likely to be repeated, because ...

Figure 6.3 A fear of heights (acrophobia) is a fairly common phobia

APPLYING CONDITIONING PROCEDURES TO THE TREATMENT OF PHOBIAS

Both classical and operant conditioning can be applied to a variety of different behaviours. The principles of both have successfully been used to help people who have psychological problems, in particular in the treatment of phobias.

A phobia is a mental illness where a person experiences extreme anxiety and fear about a particular stimulus object, for example the outdoors (agoraphobia) or small spaces (claustrophobia). Phobias can affect a person's everyday life; for example, they may not be able to hold down a job because they may come across their phobia, friends and family may stop visiting because they don't understand their problem or think that their problem is a bit weird.

The therapies that we will look at use the principles of classical and operant conditioning.

Behaviour therapy and classical conditioning

This treatment is based on the principle that behaviour (such as fear) is a response to a stimulus (the phobia); for example, an arachnophobic (somebody who is scared of spiders) when faced with a spider will experience the fear response (heart rate increasing, breathing increasing, sweating etc.). Treatment requires getting rid of that fear response (extinction) as outlined in the three methods described below.

Systematic desensitisation

In systematic desensitisation the person with the phobia (the phobic) is exposed very gradually to the feared stimulus.

To begin with, the phobic and the therapist create a 'hierarchy of fear' together. This is a list of increasingly fearful situations, starting with one that the phobic can tolerate and ending with one that would create the most intense fear. Using the example of a fear of spiders, a hierarchy could be:

Step 1 (least fearful situation)	Looking at the word spider.
Step 2	Looking at a video of a spider.
Step 3	Seeing a spider in a glass box on the other side of the room.
Step 4	Touching the spider in the box.
Step 5 (most fearful situation)	Holding the spider in their hand.

The hierarchies will obviously be different for each person.

Figure 6.4 After systematic desensitisation even a person with a fear of spiders (arachnophobia) can endure a close encounter with the feared stimulus

The phobic is then taught relaxation techniques and, when completely relaxed, experiences the first stage of the hierarchy of fearful situations (looking at the word in this case). When they are comfortable with that level of exposure, they move to the next stage.

The phobic does not move to the next fearful situation until they feel ready. If they become fearful, treatment returns to the previous stage. Finally, they are able to handle the most feared situation comfortably: the phobia is extinguished.

ACTIVITY

Write a five-step hierarchy for somebody who is scared of heights.

This method is thought to work because it seems unlikely that humans can experience fear and relaxation at the same time. Therefore, the stimulus (the spider) cannot trigger the phobic response (fear).

- Systematic desensitisation is generally successful in treating specific phobias (of an animal or an object) but is less so for more general phobias such as fear of open spaces (agoraphobia).
- It is more suitable for use with children than the techniques described below.
- Ethical concerns are few, because the patient plays such an active part in the structure and pace of the treatment (the patient is responsible for writing the hierarchy and if they feel that they aren't completely happy with one of the stages, they don't move onto the next one until they are comfortable). However, this can be problematic as the treatment may take an extended period of time and the phobic may fail to complete it if they feel they are not progressing.

Flooding

Flooding is based on the idea that the human body cannot maintain the fear response for a prolonged period (that is, a person cannot experience the fear response for a long period of time – the body will not allow it). In contrast to the previous method, the phobic is confronted with their most intense fearful situation straight away: there is no gradual exposure to it. The procedure for flooding is:

- The phobic is exposed to the feared stimulus (for example looking out over the top of a tall building). The phobic experiences an intense fear response
- This situation is maintained, the phobic cannot escape and the response continues. The phobic may show intense mental and physical distress. They are told to stay with the phobic stimulus (for example, keep looking)
- Eventually the response becomes exhausted because the body cannot maintain that level of physiological arousal (fear); the phobic remains in the feared situation but does not show the fear response as it has become extinguished.

ACTIVITY

Using the 'fear of crowds' phobia, suggest a way that a person could receive flooding treatment for it.

EVALUATION BOX

- The evidence suggests that this technique is the most successful.
- It is quicker and cheaper than systematic desensitisation.
- However, it does raise ethical concerns, as the therapist takes considerable responsibility for the phobic's well-being.
- The therapist may have to act against the wishes of the phobic, as expressed during the flooding process.
- However, before the phobic takes part, the full procedure and the phobic's likely response should be explained. Usually the phobic is given time to think about the treatment before they decide to go ahead with it. This is why these techniques are not appropriate for children, who cannot fully understand how they will feel, nor be in a position to give informed consent.

ACTIVITY

Outline three differences between systematic desensitisation and flooding, using the table below.

	Systematic desensitisation	Flooding
How does it work?		
Length of therapy		
Ethical issues		

Systematic desensitisation and flooding both use the principles of classical conditioning, as the aim is to change the response from fear to a response of being calm. Before therapy, the client associates the fearful stimulus (for example, a spider) with a fearful response. After therapy the client associates the fearful stimulus with a calm response. They have learnt through association.

Aversion therapy

The purpose of aversion therapy is to stop unwanted behaviour by associating it (through conditioning) with something unpleasant.

Aversion therapy has been used to treat alcoholics, using the classical conditioning procedure as illustrated below.

- The alcoholic is given a drug that makes them feel sick. The drug is the unconditioned stimulus and the nausea the unconditioned response
- The patient is then given a drink of alcohol and the drug (so the two are paired together) and feels sick
- This pairing occurs several times until the alcohol (the conditioned stimulus) becomes associated with nausea (which has become the conditioned response), so the patient no longer drinks alcohol.

	Stimulus	Response
The situation before the condition starts	Drug (UCS) Alcohol	Nausea (UCR) No response (no nausea)
During treatment	Drug and alcohol	Nausea
When conditioning has occurred	Alcohol (CS)	Nausea (CR)

EVALUATION BOX

- The success rate for aversion therapy is mixed depending on the person. It seems to be more effective for some people than others.
- One difficulty is that if the pairing does not continue occasionally, the association will become extinguished and the alcoholic may return to drink. The only way to avoid this is for the alcoholic to stay away from alcohol.
- There are ethical concerns over this method because of the effects on the patient and the responsibility on the therapist. As in the previous method, the alcoholic is given very detailed information about what the treatment entails and what they might experience. Usually they are given time to think about this before they decide to have the treatment; they may need ongoing support if it is to be successful.

Operant conditioning

Token economy

The purpose of a 'token economy' is also to change unwanted behaviour (for example not eating due to anorexia nervosa, or naughty behaviour in class).

The token economy uses the principles of operant conditioning: it uses reinforcement to change a person's behaviour. Desired behaviour is rewarded with tokens that can be exchanged for something that the individual wants.

The token economy is used mostly in institutional settings such as psychiatric hospitals where a fixed tariff (an agreement between the doctors and patients) is awarded for good behaviour. An example in the case of anorexia might be to receive a token for eating a certain amount of calories; the tokens can then be used to buy desired rewards (perhaps ten tokens to watch a video or have friends come to visit).

ACTIVITY

Teachers and parents use the principles of the token economy with young children. List five ways in which they do this.

EVALUATION BOX

- The token economy has been found to be very effective for managing patients and improving their self-care and social skills.
- It requires close monitoring of patient behaviour for it to work, however, and patients tend to become very dependent on the system, making it difficult for them once they leave the institution.

THE ETHICS OF CONDITIONING PROCEDURES

We have looked at some applications of conditioning and evaluated them. However, there are also some important ethical concerns to consider.

Ethical issues are there to protect the well-being of the people that are taking part in research or, in this case, the treatment process. The issues must be considered before they take part and any issues need to be outlined. If any problems occur during the treatment, they must be addressed afterwards. The ethical issues for conditioning procedures are as follows:

- Although behaviour is changed, the underlying causes of that behaviour are not addressed. As a result, these procedures may create a new kind of faulty behaviour in the patient. The patient may learn to be frightened of another object as a result of therapy (for example, if they are scared of heights and, on their way up a tall building, have to get in a lift, they may then become fearful of lifts)

- Some of these techniques allow vulnerable people to be controlled by those who are more powerful, and this power may be abused (for example, the therapist may cause distress to the client)
- Basic ethical issues of informed consent, right to withdraw and preventing distress are all raised by the use of these procedures. Patients must be aware of exactly what is going to happen in the procedures and give their consent to take part. They should also have the right to withdraw from the treatment if they wish, if it all becomes too much for them. Distress (mental and physical) should be avoided at all costs.

EXAM STYLE QUESTIONS

Read the information in the table below, which describes attempts to apply conditioning procedures to phobias. Decide which type of treatment it is describing: aversion therapy, flooding, token economy or systematic desensitisation.

Description	Treatment
Geoffrey is scared of heights. He is taken to the top of the Empire State building in New York to conquer his fear.	
Gillian is given a box of chocolates every time she faces her fear.	
Lesley is trying to quit drinking alcohol. He has been taught to associate pain (an electric shock) with drinking alcohol.	
Ceri has been taught relaxation techniques and gradually faces her fear of dogs. Step by step, Ceri is gradually learning to overcome her fear of dogs.	

TEST YOURSELF

1   Which therapies are based on operant conditioning principles?
2   Which therapies are based on classical conditioning principles?
3   In your own words, explain how flooding therapy works.
4   In your own words, explain how aversion therapy works.
5   Suggest one situation in which a token economy may be effective.
6   Outline two ethical problems that may arise when using therapies based on conditioning.

Social influence

WHAT YOU NEED TO KNOW FOR THE EXAMINATION

What you need to know for the examination:

- Conformity – its definition, description and evaluation of studies, and explanation of factors affecting conformity
- Obedience – its definition, description and evaluation of studies, and explanation of factors affecting obedience
- Social loafing – its definition, description and evaluation of studies, and explanation of factors affecting social loafing

- Deindividuation – its definition, description and evaluation of studies, and explanation of factors affecting deindividuation
- Bystander behaviour – description and evaluation of studies including those of Latané and Darley (1968), Bateson (1983), Piliavin (1969) and Schroeder (1995); explanation of factors affecting bystander behaviour
- Contemporary practical implications of research into social influence

How does other people's behaviour affect yours? Why do you often 'go along with the crowd'? Why do we obey teachers, parents and other figures of authority?

Psychologists call this particular part of psychology social influence: it concerns how other people affect our behaviour.

Have you ever put your hand up in class when asked to vote for something, not really knowing what your view is, but everybody else has their hand up? By doing this you are conforming to the norms of the group. Would you ever hurt another human being if a stranger in a white lab coat told you to? Research by Stanley Milgram supported the idea that the atrocities in Nazi Germany could have been performed by many of us. This chapter looks at some of the research that has tried to discover how and why other people influence our behaviour.

Figure 7.1 Adolf Hitler was regarded as a figure of authority

CONFORMITY

ACTIVITY

Do you always make your own decisions? Ask yourself what the reason might be for:

• Laughing at a joke that you don't find funny or understand because everyone else is laughing
• Looking around at other people in a restaurant if you don't know which knife and fork to use
• Buying the latest fashion because all of your friends are wearing it.

KEY TERM

Conformity – a change in belief or behaviour due to real or imagined group pressure.

All of the situations above are examples of conformity.

Although many of us like to think that we make our own decisions, in reality we often conform by changing our behaviour or opinions so that they fit in with those of other people in a group (whether it be friends or strangers). This is known as conformity, which can be defined as a change in belief or behaviour due to real or imagined group pressure.

EXAM STYLE QUESTIONS

Outline what is meant by the term conformity.

Explanations of factors affecting conformity

When you completed the first activity, were your answers something like:

- To fit in, to be liked, to be accepted, or to not be ridiculed
- Because you are unsure of how to act, or the other people in the group might know more?

These are two ways to explain conformity; these are known as normative social influence and informational social influence.

KEY TERMS

Normative social influence – when we want to be liked by the other people in a group: we want to feel accepted by them and not be left out.

Informational social influence – using the behaviour of the people around us for information when we are in an ambiguous situation and are unsure of how to act. We might regard these people as 'experts' and may copy their behaviour.

ACTIVITY

Which examples in the first activity explain normative social influence?

ACTIVITY

Which examples in the first explain informational social influence?

Can you think of any other examples of when you have conformed?

Conformity can have both good and bad consequences; can you think of an example for each?

EXAM STYLE QUESTIONS

Using your knowledge of psychology, outline two reasons why people conform.

Research into conformity

KEY STUDY

Asch (1951)

Aim: To find out if an individual would conform to the group even if they knew the group was wrong.

Method: Solomon Asch devised a number of laboratory experiments with groups of six to nine participants (all male college students). There was one naive participant and the rest were confederates who had been told to give wrong answers on certain trials.

KEY TERM

Confederate: an accomplice of the investigator who pretends to be a participant during an experiment.

KEY STUDY – (continued)

The task was for participants to judge the length of lines (they were told that it was a test of visual perception – this is an element of deception). Asch showed the groups lines of different lengths (see Figure 7.2) and asked them to match the test line to one of the comparison lines (A, B or C). As you can see, the answer is clearly obvious. The participant was one of the last to give his judgement.

Results: In control groups trials, when participants were tested alone (and so there was no pressure to conform), there were very few wrong answers. But Asch found that when they became part of a group, 25 per cent of participants conformed to the rest of the group on most of the occasions when the group was wrong. Overall, 75 percent of participants conformed to the wrong answer at least once. The average rate of conformity was 32 per cent.

Conclusion: Asch concluded that the participants' behaviour is representative of conformity. Participants conformed to fit into the group and not be ridiculed, even though the people in the group were strangers.

RESEARCH METHODS

The Asch experiment is an example of a laboratory experiment. A description of a laboratory experiment and its strengths and weaknesses can be found in Chapter 5: Research methods and ethics – part 1, pages 70–71.

ASK YOURSELF

Why do you think Asch made the answer so obvious?

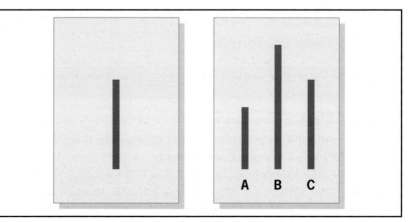

Figure 7.2 As you can see, the line on the left is clearly the same length as line C

ACTIVITY

Using the results of the Asch experiment, draw a bar chart to display the percentages described above. Provide a suitable title and fully label your bar chart.

ACTIVITY

Using the explanations of normative social influence and informational social influence, can you explain the behaviour of Asch's participants?

When participants were interviewed afterwards and debriefed, most of them said that they knew they were giving the wrong answer but, for example, did not want to look foolish or 'upset the experiment' (this is known as demand characteristics). In further trials, Asch found that the following factors influenced conformity:

- Group size – levels of conformity were affected by the number of people in the group; however, conformity does not increase in groups larger than four, so it is considered the optimal group size
- Anonymity – when participants could write their answers down as opposed to announcing them publicly, conformity levels dropped. This suggests that individuals conform because they are concerned about what other people think of them
- Unanimity – when one other person in the group gave a different answer to the others, and therefore the group answer was not unanimous, conformity dropped. This was true even if that person's answer also seemed to be wrong.

ACTIVITY

Below are some evaluation points for you to consider with regards to Asch's research. Try to complete and develop each point.

1 The participants were **deceived**: this is unethical because …
2 The participants were confused and embarrassed during the investigation. This is unethical because …
3 The method used was a **laboratory experiment**. This is an advantage because … This is a disadvantage because …
4 White, American, male college students were used in the original study. This is a limitation because …
5 The nature of the task was artificial. This is a disadvantage because …

EVALUATION BOX

- Participants were deceived about the true nature of the investigation: they were told it was a study on perceptual judgement. However, the deception was necessary: if they had been told it was a study of conformity the behaviour wouldn't have been natural and participants might have displayed demand characteristics.
- The participants were confused and embarrassed. It is wrong to cause participants any physical or psychological pain. This ethical guideline is known as the protection of participants.
- The method used was a laboratory experiment. An advantage of this is that variables can be controlled and it can be easily replicated (Asch did several variations of his original experiment). A disadvantage is that laboratory experiments lack ecological validity: this means that the findings cannot be generalised to other people, places or settings.
- The sample only consisted of white, American, male college students, which means that it is not a representative sample. Would women have conformed as much as the men? What about people who weren't in education?
- The nature of the task was artificial. It is not an everyday task to judge the length of lines, so it could be argued that both the task and the behaviour were artificial.

Practical implications of research into conformity

Why people conform and why others refuse to conform is an important question in society. Law makers and those that uphold and implement the law, such as the police, must encourage a degree of conformity; knowing how to do this and how best to proceed in certain situations is extremely useful.

It is also very useful for politicians and others who hope to change people's minds and encourage people to think in a certain way – for example, to save energy and water, or to recycle more – to know how best to do this.

EXAM STYLE QUESTIONS

Describe and evaluate one study into conformity; try to include the method, results, conclusion and an evaluation point.

TEST YOURSELF

1 What is conformity?
2 What is normative social influence?
3 Give an example of when you conformed due to normative social influence.
4 What is informational social influence?
5 Give an example of when you conformed due to informational social influence.
6 In psychological research, what is a confederate?
7 What was the aim of the Asch study?
8 In the Asch study, how were the participants deceived?
9 What were the results of the Asch study?
10 What can you conclude about the Asch study?
11 Outline one strength and one weakness of the Asch study.

ASK YOURSELF

If a policeman asked you to pick up a piece of litter off the street, would you do it?

If a person wearing jeans and a T-shirt asked you to do the same, would you?

Why do we obey figures of authority? What are the consequences if we don't?

OBEDIENCE

Doing what a figure of authority asks is known as obedience.

KEY TERM

Obedience – following an order, instruction or command which is given by a figure of authority.

EXAM STYLE QUESTIONS

Outline what is meant by the term obedience.

One of the most famous pieces of psychological research into obedience was conducted by Stanley Milgram.

ASK YOURSELF

How is obedience different from conformity?

What do you think the benefits can be of obedience in society?

Can you think of any atrocities that have occurred which involved people obeying figures of authority?

Research into obedience

KEY STUDY

Milgram (1963)

Aim: Milgram was interested in discovering why so many Germans were obedient to the Nazi authority figures during World War II. He wanted to test obedience in an American setting.

Method: He advertised in a local paper for male volunteers between the ages of 20 and 50 years to take part in a study of learning at Yale University. He then selected his participants from the volunteers.

When the participants arrived at Yale University, they were introduced to Mr Wallace, who unbeknown to them was a **confederate**. They were told that they were to be paired with Mr Wallace and that one would play the role of the teacher, and one would play the role of the learner, and that they would pick these roles out of a hat (it was actually fixed so that Mr Wallace was always the learner).

An experimenter (who was wearing a grey lab coat) took them into a room and strapped Mr Wallace into a chair and placed some electrodes on his arms. The teacher was told that Mr Wallace had a mild heart condition. The experimenter and the teacher then went into an adjoining room and the teacher was shown the shock 'generator' (see Figure 7.3). This contained a row of switches ranging from 15 volts (slight shock) to 450 volts (XXX). The teacher did not know that the shock 'generator' was fake. The only real shock that took place was when the teacher was given a 45-volt shock to make the whole procedure convincing.

The teacher was then told that the procedure for the investigation was to be for him to read out a number of word pairs, which the learner had to remember. If the learner gave an incorrect answer, or did not say anything, the teacher had to shock him (with the shock increasing each time by 15 volts).

The whole experiment was **standardised** so that all participants experienced the same procedure, and so that it allowed for a fair test.

The learner got the first few answers correct and then started to make mistakes. At 180 volts, the learner shouted that he could

KEY STUDY – (continued)

not stand the pain, at 300 volts he banged on the wall and begged the teacher to stop, and at 315 volts, there was silence. Despite this, the teachers still continued to shock the learner as he wasn't giving them an answer.

The participants were seen to sweat, tremble, and bite their lips; three participants even had a seizure during the experiment. A lot of them asked the experimenter if he could check to see if Mr Wallace was OK. The experimenter responded with a number of predetermined prods, such as: 'The experiment requires that you continue.' and: 'Although the shocks are painful, there is no permanent tissue damage.'

Results: Before Milgram started the experiment, he asked some psychiatrists to predict how many people they thought would administer the 450 volts, and they, like Milgram, predicted around 2 per cent. The actual results were that all participants administered 300 volts, and 65 per cent delivered 450 volts.

When the experiment had ended, by either the participant refusing to continue or they had reached the final voltage, they were **debriefed**. They were introduced again to Mr Wallace and told the real reason for the experiment. They were assured that their behaviour was normal.

Conclusion: Milgram concluded that people will obey a figure of authority, even if it means hurting another person.

RESEARCH METHODS

The Milgram study is an example of a laboratory experiment. A description of a laboratory experiment and its strengths and weaknesses can be found in Chapter 5: Research methods and ethics – part 1, pages 70–71.

ACTIVITY

Name the sampling method that was used in this study. Name one advantage and one disadvantage of using this type of sample.

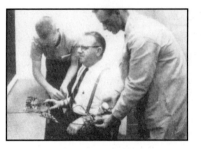 

Figure 7.3 Milgram's 'learner' having the electrodes strapped on and the participant receiving a sample shock from the generator

When Milgram followed up the participants a year later, 82 per cent of them said that they were glad to have taken part, and that they had learnt a great deal about themselves; 1 per cent of them said that they deeply regretted it and the rest were of a neutral opinion.

ACTIVITY

Write one open and one closed question that Milgram could have asked the participants in the follow-up interviews.

Explanations of factors affecting levels of obedience

Milgram was surprised by his results and was interested to discover why so many people did follow the orders. He conducted some more research where he changed a few of the variables to see if they affected the levels of obedience.

ACTIVITY

Read the variations of the Milgram experiment below. Say whether you think the obedience levels would be higher or lower than 65 per cent and give a reason why:

- The setting was moved from Yale (a prestigious American university) to a run-down office
- The experimenter left the room during the experiment and told the teacher to continue with the shocks
- The experimenter gave orders via telephone
- The teacher and learner were in the same room
- The experimenter was not wearing a lab coat and did not appear to be a figure of authority
- The teacher had to force the learner's hand onto a shock plate.

In all variations, the obedience levels dropped. Let's have a look why:

- **Prestige** – when the setting was moved to a run-down office, obedience levels dropped as the original study was conducted at a very prestigious university
- **Surveillance** – when the experimenter left the room, and also when he gave orders via telephone, obedience level dropped. Participants were less likely to follow the orders as they didn't have the physical presence of the experimenter there
- **Buffers** – this is anything that prevents those who obey from being aware of the full impact of their actions. In the original study the wall was a buffer between the teacher and the learner; when they were both in the same room, obedience levels dropped
- **Authority** – when the experimenter didn't appear as a figure of authority and wasn't wearing a lab coat, obedience levels dropped. Milgram suggested that when individuals perceive another person as having authority over them, they no longer feel responsible for their actions ('I was told to do it') and become an agent of the authority
- **Personal responsibility** – when the participant had to force the learner's hand onto the shock plate, he had more responsibility for his suffering and so obedience level dropped.

EXAM STYLE QUESTIONS

Using your knowledge of psychology, outline two reasons why people obey a figure of authority.

ACTIVITY

Below are some evaluation points for you to consider with regard to Milgram's research. Try to complete and develop each point.

1 The participants suffered distress during the experiment. Three of them had seizures. This is unethical because ...
2 Only white, American men were used in the investigation. This is a limitation because ...
3 The method used was a **laboratory experiment**. This is an advantage because ... This is a disadvantage because ...
4 Participants were **deceived**. This is unethical because ...

EVALUATION BOX

1 The participants suffered distress during the experiment and three of them had seizures. It is unethical to cause this much distress to participants and the experiment should have been stopped; however, Milgram argued that there was no way that he could have predicted the results.
2 The sample cannot be generalised to women and people in other cultures as he only used white, American men; however, when he replicated the study with women, the obedience levels were the same as for the men in the original study.
3 The method used was a laboratory experiment. An advantage of this is that it can be replicated (which Milgram did) and the variables can be controlled. The disadvantages include the fact that it is an artificial environmental and task (you are not asked to electrocute people every day), so the study lacks ecological validity, which means that it cannot be generalised to other people, places and settings.
4 Participants were deceived as to the true nature of the investigation, also to the fact that Mr Wallace was a confederate and that the shocks weren't real; however, deception was necessary as, if they had known the real aim of the investigation, there wouldn't have been any point in doing it.

EXAM STYLE QUESTIONS

Describe and evaluate one study into obedience; try to include the method, results, conclusion and an evaluation point.

ACTIVITY

Answer the following questions:

1 Do you think that the Milgram study would be allowed to be conducted today? Why?
2 What does it tell us about obedience?
3 Were the Nazis in World War II different, or is any human being capable of doing this?

Practical implications of research into obedience

Knowledge of how and why people are obedient in different situations is extremely useful in helping us to understand individuals' behaviour, for example why the soldiers in charge of the Nazi death camps did what they did. As Philip Zimbardo says, while their behaviour was in no way acceptable, it is understandable.

Unfortunately, the lessons that should have been learned from World War II seemed to have passed us by: news about Abhu Ghraib prison in Iraq, for instance, where soldiers acting as guards behaved extremely badly to Iraqi prisoners, is chilling evidence that human beings can do the most terrible things in certain circumstances.

TEST YOURSELF

1 What is meant by the term obedience?
2 Outline one difference between conformity and obedience.
3 What was the aim of the Milgram study?
4 How were the participants deceived in the Milgram study?
5 The naive participant always played the role of the teacher. Why were the roles of the teacher and learner always fixed?
6 Why was the whole procedure standardised (the confederate's answers and responses were the same for all of the participants and the experimenter used the same prods)?
7 What were the results of the Milgram study? How many participants went up to 300 volts? How many participants went up to 450 volts?
8 What did Milgram and psychiatrists originally predict about how many participants would deliver the full 450 volts?
9 Name three of the variations of the original experiment and say how these affected the levels of obedience.
10 How can Milgram's results be used to explain obedience?

Have you ever noticed that when you are working in a group, compared with working alone, each individual tends to reduce their own effort?

Can you think of an example where you have done this?

KEY TERM

Social loafing – when people put less effort into a task that is being performed with others.

SOCIAL LOAFING

Max Ringelmann (1913) conducted an investigation with men playing a tug-of-war task and concluded that the greater the number of men involved, the less effort each individual put in.

This is known as the Ringelmann effect and it forms part of the concept of social loafing.

KEY STUDY

Latané *et al.* (1979)

Aim: To test the idea of social loafing.

Method: Participants were split into two conditions that involved them shouting and clapping loudly. In one condition they were on their own; in another they were with four or six other people. Participants had to wear headsets so that they didn't know how much noise the others were making. Investigators recorded the amount of noise that was made.

Results: The results showed that the more people there were in the group, the less was the effort made by each individual. The output of sound when working with five others was reduced to about one-third of their output when alone.

Conclusion: The participants made less effort in groups because other people were contributing to the task. This is an example of social loafing.

RESEARCH METHODS

The Latané *et al.* study is an example of a laboratory experiment. A description of a laboratory experiment and its strengths and weaknesses can be found in Chapter 5: Research methods and ethics – part 1, pages 70–71.

Bibb Latané *et al.* suggested that the identification of an individual's effort in a group task eliminates the effects of social loafing. They also suggested that the reason for the results of the noise study was because participants thought that their own effort could not be measured.

ASK YOURSELF

What does this suggest about other people influencing our behaviour?

EXAM STYLE QUESTIONS

Outline what is meant by the term social loafing.

EVALUATION BOX

- Most of the research has taken place in a laboratory setting using artificial tasks; therefore, the studies can be said to lack ecological validity. Participants would behave differently in a real-life setting. Being asked to clap while wearing headphones is not an everyday occurrence.
- Participants may display **demand characteristics** as they are performing in front of the researchers and so may pick up cues as to how they should act.

Practical implications of research into social loafing

Knowledge of factors influencing social loafing can be useful when managing teams of people, perhaps in the armed forces, or in less physical environments such as a busy office. Knowing how to distribute tasks to a workforce and how the workforce will respond is an extremely important and valuable management skill, and can mean the difference between the success and failure of an organisation!

EXAM STYLE QUESTIONS

Describe and evaluate one study into social loafing; try to include the method, results, conclusion and an evaluation point.

EXAM STYLE QUESTIONS

Look at the examples of social behaviour below and state whether each is an example of social loafing, conformity or obedience:

1 Mary tidies her bedroom because her mother has told her to.
2 Joshua likes doing group work in class because he doesn't have to do as much work as he thinks the rest of the group will.
3 Ryan goes to the cinema to see a film that he doesn't really want to see, but all of his friends are going to watch it.

DEINDIVIDUATION

This is known as deindividuation. A definition of it is: 'the loss of self-awareness and sense of personal responsibility that occurs in members of a crowd'.

EXAM STYLE QUESTIONS

Define what is meant by the term deindividuation.

This may occur because we may feel anonymous in a crowd and so have fewer restraints on our behaviour. We are more likely to be impulsive and follow the behaviour of those around us.

When you were asked above about what you would do if you were invisible for the day, how many of your acts were antisocial?

KEY STUDY

Zimbardo (1969)

Aim: To test the idea of deindividuation.

Method: Using female participants in groups of four, participants had to give electric shocks to Philip Zimbardo's confederates.

The participants believed that they were taking part in a learning exercise. There were two conditions: in one the women wore hoods and identical coats (so that they were anonymous); in the other they wore their own clothes with name tags on and spoke to each other using their own names.

Results: Zimbardo found that the anonymous women were twice as likely to give shocks compared with the women wearing their own clothes.

Conclusion: Zimbardo concluded that if people know that they cannot be identified (have anonymity) they are more likely to behave aggressively.

RESEARCH METHODS

The Zimbardo study is an example of a laboratory experiment. A description of a laboratory experiment and its strengths and weaknesses can be found in Chapter 5: Research methods and ethics – part 1, pages 70–71.

EVALUATION BOX

- The method used was a laboratory experiment. An advantage of this is that it can be replicated and the variables can be controlled. The disadvantages include the fact that it is an artificial environment and task (you are not asked to electrocute people every day, especially wearing hoods and coats) and also the study lacks ecological validity, which means that it cannot be generalised to other people, places and settings.
- The participants may have experienced distress. It is unethical to cause participants psychological harm.

KEY STUDY

Diener et al. (1976)

Aim: To test the idea that if people are anonymous (cannot be identified), they are likely to commit antisocial acts.

Method: They asked 27 women to give out sweets to 1,000 trick-or-treaters during Halloween night. There were two conditions: in one the children were asked for their names and addresses (identifiable); in the other the children remained anonymous. While the women were chatting to the children, their phone rang and so they went to answer it. The women left the children at the door with the instruction to take one sweet each. A hidden observer recorded whether the children stole any additional sweets.

Results: The children were more likely to steal when they were anonymous.

Conclusion: E. Diener et al. concluded that people are more likely to steal when they cannot be identified.

RESEARCH METHODS

The Diener et al. study is an example of a field experiment. A description of a field experiment and its strengths and weaknesses can be found in Chapter 5: Research methods and ethics – part 1, pages 71–72.

EVALUATION BOX

The Diener *et al.* study is a field experiment, which means that most of the variables can be controlled and it is fairly easy to replicate. Because participants don't always know that they are taking part in an investigation (which makes consent an issue) they display more natural behaviour. Also, as the setting is a real-life one, it has higher ecological validity, so the findings can be generalised to other settings.

EXAM STYLE QUESTIONS

Describe and evaluate one study into deindividuation; try to include the method, results, conclusion and an evaluation point.

Draw up a table showing the similarities and differences between a lab and a field experiment.

Explanation of factors affecting deindividuation

So, what factors affect deindividuation?

- **The mood of the crowd** – when people are in a crowd they tend to pick up the mood and respond to it (for example, football hooliganism could be explained in this way). It can also have a positive effect (for example, people dancing at a concert).
- **Anonymity** – this is supported by the research by Zimbardo and Diener *et al.* If participants are anonymous, they are more likely to engage in antisocial behaviour. Leon Mann (1981) examined a range of newspaper articles about the behaviour of people in crowds who had watched somebody threatening to commit suicide, for example by jumping from a building. He noticed that, shockingly, on some occasions the crowds had tried to encourage the individuals to jump. This occurred when the crowd was large, when it was dark and when they weren't close to the person attempting to jump.

ASK YOURSELF

What does this suggest?

Practical implications of research into deindividuation

Research into deindividuation suggests that people cease to behave as individuals when in crowds. The implications are that the normal, acceptable rules and norms of society change when people are in crowds or when they conform to large groups by wearing uniforms or the same sports kit.

When crowds gather, we often find police present and tension building. Political rallies and marches often end in aggressive confrontation. Knowledge of deindividuation can help the police to deal with crowd situations, by splitting the crowd into smaller units, and building and maintaining calm while the crowd disperses; the police themselves can also behave extremely aggressively and violently to those protesting, however, because they themselves are uniformed and are, to some extent, deindividuated.

The US Army has applied the knowledge and principles of deindividuation to its rules governing the behaviour of troops who are on leave or who leave the army permanently. It used to be the case that soldiers could take their uniforms with them when they left, but now wearing a uniform is only allowed on special occasions. This is because the US Army believes that with the uniform comes a sense of deindividuation and, as such, the soldier may be attacked as an 'army member' rather than an individual. Also, the soldier may feel disinhibited by their uniform and act irresponsibly, bringing the army into disrepute.

ASK YOURSELF

Are you a helpful person? Can you give an example of when you last helped somebody?

Imagine you are on a bus and a blind man carrying a white stick gets on. After a few minutes he falls over. Would you help him? Would you be as helpful if a person that was drunk fell in front of you?

You would probably be more likely to help the blind person than the drunk, but why?

TEST YOURSELF

1 Outline what is meant by the term 'deindividuation'?
2 State one example of when this might occur from the research evidence above.
3 What did Zimbardo's research suggest about deindividuation?
4 What did Diener *et al.*'s research suggest about deindividuation?
5 Which study displays more natural behaviour and why?
6 What are the two factors that can affect deindividuation?

BYSTANDER BEHAVIOUR

Bibb Latané and John Darley were the first psychologists to start research into bystander behaviour after they were shocked and confused by a murder in the USA. Kitty Genovese was assaulted several times very early one morning by a man. Her cries for help ('Help, he's just stabbed me') woke the people living in the area where she was being assaulted. In the space of 30 minutes her attacker continued to assault her before eventually returning to kill her. The police found that 38 people living nearby had either seen or heard the attack but that no one had helped.

Why didn't anybody help Kitty? We would probably like to think that we would help, but psychologists have put forward a number of different explanations that might suggest otherwise. These explanations attempt to explain bystander behaviour. This term covers two different concepts: bystander apathy (when a bystander does not help the person in need) and bystander intervention (when a person does help the person in need).

EXAM STYLE QUESTIONS

Outline what is meant by the term bystander behaviour.

Explanation of factors affecting bystander behaviour

Latané and Darley wanted to test this idea. They believed that as the number of bystanders increases, the less likely the victim is to get help. This is a concept called diffusion of responsibility.

KEY STUDY

Latané and Darley (1968)

Aim: To test the concept of diffusion of responsibility.

Method: They tested this concept by asking students to sit in booths and communicate with each other via an intercom. They had a number of different conditions, which were as follows:

1 The participant believed that there was only one other person in the booth.
2 The participant believed that there were two other people in the booth.
3 The participant believed that there were five other people in the booth.

After the discussion had started, one of the others (a confederate) mentioned that he was epileptic. After a few minutes, he pretended that he was having a seizure.

ASK YOURSELF

Why do you think this was the case? Would you have helped?

KEY TERMS

Bystander behaviour – bystander apathy and bystander intervention.

Bystander apathy – when a bystander does not help the person in need.

Bystander intervention – when a bystander does help the person in need.

Diffusion of responsibility – the more bystanders that witness an incident, the less likely it is that one of them will help.

ASK YOURSELF

Do you think the size of the group of bystanders has an effect on whether they will help or not?

KEY STUDY – (continued)

Results:

Condition	Percentage of participants that responded within the first four minutes
The participant believed that there was only one other person in the booth.	85%
The participant believed that there were two other people in the booth.	62%
The participant believed that there were five other people in the booth.	31%

Conclusion: When the participant thought that they were alone with the confederate, they were far more likely to help, compared with the participants who believed that they were in a larger group. This is an example of diffusion of responsibility, which supports the idea that as the number of bystanders increases, the less chance the victim has of receiving help, as the responsibility for the help is shared or diffused among them all.

RESEARCH METHODS

The Latané and Darley study is an example of a laboratory experiment. A description of a laboratory experiment and its strengths and weaknesses can be found in Chapter 5: Research methods and ethics – part 1, pages 70–71.

ACTIVITY

Draw a bar chart to represent this data. Be sure to give it an appropriate title and label the axis.

ACTIVITY

How would you investigate diffusion of responsibility?

Another explanation put forward to explain bystander behaviour is called pluralistic ignorance. In ambiguous situations (unknown or unclear), people often look to others for help in terms of what to do. In an emergency situation, if all other bystanders are also unsure of what to do, it is likely that this will have an effect on everybody else, and hence produce the wrong guidance.

This concept was effectively demonstrated by Latané and Darley again, in a well-known study called 'the smoke-filled room'.

KEY STUDY

Latané and Darley (1968)

Aim: To test the concept of pluralistic ignorance.

Method: There were two conditions. In the first condition participants were asked to sit in a room and complete a questionnaire on the pressures of urban life. The experimenter then arranged for smoke (actually steam) to pour into the room through a vent in the wall. The participants were watched through a one-way mirror and were timed as to how long it took them to report the smoke. The experiment was stopped after six minutes.

In the second condition the procedure was as above, but participants were in a group with two confederates. When the participant asked them what they thought was happening, they replied 'Dunno' to all questions.

Results: Only 10 per cent reported the smoke within six minutes when there were passive others in the room (compared with 75 per cent when alone).

Conclusion: This is a clear example of pluralistic ignorance. People didn't want to overreact in the presence of others. We use their behaviour as guidance: if they appear to be calm, then there mustn't be a problem.

ASK YOURSELF

How can you apply diffusion of responsibility to the case of Kitty Genovese?

KEY TERM

Pluralistic ignorance – When each bystander takes no action and thus misleads the others into defining the incident as a non-emergency.

RESEARCH METHODS

The Latané and Darley study is an example of a field experiment. A description of a field experiment and its strengths and weaknesses can be found in Chapter 5: Research methods and ethics – part 1, pages 71–72.

ACTIVITY

Why might pluralistic ignorance sometimes lead to a disaster?

EXAM STYLE QUESTIONS

Read the following examples and state whether they are an example of pluralistic ignorance or diffusion of responsibility:

- Bob drives past a person who has broken down on the motorway; he doesn't stop because he thinks that other people will stop and help
- Janice isn't worried when the fire alarm goes off at work because nobody else is panicking.

Using your knowledge of psychology, outline what is meant by the terms 'diffusion of responsibility' and 'pluralistic ignorance'.

ASK YOURSELF

What do you think the costs of helping somebody are? Would this make you less likely to help them?

Think back to the question you were asked at the start of this section, where you were asked to say who you would be more likely to help, a blind or a drunken victim. No doubt you said the blind victim, as he cannot help his condition, whereas the drunken victim can. The characteristics of the victim are another concept that can also be linked to the 'costs' of helping.

Psychologists suggest that we weigh up the costs and rewards of helping somebody and, if the costs outweigh the rewards, then we are less likely to help. If it is the other way round, we will help.

Irving Piliavin *et al.* studied this concept in one of the most famous experiments in the field of psychology. The study, 'Good Samaritanism: an underground phenomenon', was conducted in 1969.

KEY STUDY

Piliavin *et al.* (1969)

Aim: To test how bystanders behaved when put in a situation where a 'victim' (a confederate) needed help. Piliavin *et al.* were also testing the concept of diffusion of responsibility.

Method: The procedure involved two male confederates playing a victim who collapsed on the subway in New York. The participants were the passengers on the train (an opportunity sample). The different conditions were as follows:

- The victim was either black or white
- The victim was either carrying a cane (blind) or appeared to be drunk
- In each condition there was a helper (confederate) who waited a certain amount of time before intervening if none of the participants did.

There were observers in the carriage who recorded how long it took people to help and if any comments were made.

Results:
- The cane victim was more likely to receive help than the other victim and was helped immediately in almost every trial regardless of his race
- The drunk victim was helped 50 per cent of the time before the helper model intervened
- The drunk victim was more likely to be helped by somebody of the same race
- The victim (who was always male) was more likely to be helped by males than females
- The number of bystanders had little effect on the rate of helping (so no diffusion of responsibility).

Conclusion: Piliavin suggested that the cost of helping is a factor affecting bystander behaviour. The person will help if the costs are low (for example, time, danger, inconvenience etc.). For example, the cane victim received far more help because the costs of helping were lower than the drunk victim (for example, danger, embarrassment).

There was no evidence of pluralistic ignorance in this study.

RESEARCH METHODS

The Piliavin study is an example of a field experiment. A description of a field experiment and its strengths and weaknesses can be found in Chapter 5: Research methods and ethics – part 1, pages 71–72.

EVALUATION BOX

- Ethical issues need to be considered here as participants (the passengers) did not know that they were taking part in an experiment and so there was no consent. Also, there wouldn't have been any debriefing as the participants would have got off the train and gone about their business. Protection of participants also needs to be considered. What if they didn't help? They may have felt guilty about this. What if they had been worried about the person that they did/didn't help?
- Advantages of a field experiment are that the researcher can study natural behaviour, because it is in a real-life setting; there is less chance of demand characteristics as the participants don't know that they are taking part in an experiment; and it is also higher in ecological validity.

In David Schroeder *et al.*'s (1995) book, a range of issues influencing bystander intervention are discussed. Shroeder extends the description of pluralistic ignorance, where people look hopefully towards others for guidance as to what to do in a situation, without realising that others are looking to them for exactly the same guidance. This means that when nothing is done in a situation (because people are ignorant as to how to act), those watching for guidance conclude that the situation must not be an emergency and do not act either.

Schroeder also concludes that people are less likely to intervene if they cannot decide on, or are not sure of, the type of action to undertake or the type of help to give. A person may be more likely to call an emergency service, such as the police or an ambulance, even though their own intervention may have been sufficient.

If they do decide to help, they can be very effective and can, because people are looking on for guidance, call on others to help directly once helping behaviour has been initiated.

Practical implications of research into bystander behaviour

Schroeder says that people are much more likely to begin to help if they have some training and feel more confident in the situation. The practical implication of this is that the more widely people are trained in basic medical assistance, in schools, colleges and places of work, the more likely people will feel able to intervene in an emergency and not suffer with bystander apathy.

EXAM STYLE QUESTIONS

Describe and evaluate one study into bystander behaviour; try to include the method, results, conclusion and an evaluation point.

There are many reasons why people do or don't help others in need. The explanations above have considered factors that may affect people not helping.

Daniel Bateson put forward a theory called the empathy altruism hypothesis. Altruism is a form of pro-social behaviour where the person helps another for no reward (that is, they do not benefit from the action). Some psychologists argue that this is not possible however, as there is always a reward, whether it be intrinsic (for example, feeling good about yourself) or extrinsic (praise from other people).

Bateson suggested that if we feel empathy for a person (being able to experience the emotions of another person by imagining ourselves in their position) we are more likely to help them. Bateson said that the higher the empathy, the more likely we are to help through altruism. He devised an experiment to test this hypothesis.

KEY STUDY

Bateson (1981)

Aim: To test the idea that if people felt high empathic concern for another person, they would help another person who appeared to be in distress.

Method: Participants were introduced to a confederate called Elaine. The participants were told that they were either similar to Elaine (the high-empathy condition) or dissimilar to Elaine (the low-empathy group). Participants then watched as Elaine received a number of electric shocks. After a while, Elaine

KEY STUDY – (continued)

appeared to become distressed and upset. Participants were then asked to make a decision. They could either take Elaine's place and receive the electric shocks instead of her, or leave the experiment.

Results: Those participants that were in the high-empathy condition (those who were told that they were similar to Elaine) were more likely to take Elaine's place, even when they were given the chance to leave. Those participants in the low-empathy condition (those who were told that they were dissimilar to Elaine) were more likely to leave.

Conclusion: This demonstrates how being empathic (being able to experience the emotions of another person by imagining ourselves in their position) can lead to altruistic behaviour. The higher the empathy, the more likely that altruistic behaviour will occur.

TEST YOURSELF

1 What is meant by the term bystander behaviour?
2 What is meant by 'bystander intervention'?
3 What is meant by 'bystander apathy'?
4 What event caused psychologists to research bystander behaviour?
5 What is meant by the term 'diffusion of responsibility'?
6 What was being tested in the 'smoke-filled room study'?
7 How have psychologists researched pluralistic ignorance?
8 According to Piliavin et al., which factors may affect bystander intervention?

CHAPTER 8

Sex and gender

ACTIVITY

Imagine that a close family member or good friend has just had a baby. Consider your answers to the following questions:

- What would be your first question on hearing the news that she has given birth?
- What colour Babygro would you buy if it was a girl?
- What toys would you buy it for its first birthday if was a boy?

'Is it a girl or a boy?' is one of the first questions a new parent asks. The answer will affect how the baby is treated and how the child views itself. Our society has different expectations of men and women, and the growing child soon learns what they are. But to what extent are these differences due to our biological make-up? This chapter first considers biological differences between males and females, and then reviews some explanations for how children come to adopt the attitudes and behaviours that their society considers appropriate to their sex.

Looking at the examples of aggression, hugging and language, which would you say are not appropriate (not usual in society) behaviour for males and for females?

ACTIVITY

What are the main differences between males and females in terms of the following?

Behaviour	Males and females are different in this way because…
Aggression	
Hugging friends	
Language used	

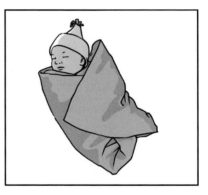

Figure 8.1 We often look at the clothing of a young baby to determine its sex. Stereotypically girls are often dressed in pink and boys in blue. A young baby dressed in yellow would lead to some confusion

BIOLOGICAL FACTORS IN SEX DIFFERENCES

Biologically there are a number of ways in which males and females differ. These are described below.

Chromosomes

The first stage in the determination of sex is the pairing of chromosomes. We have 23 pairs of chromosomes in each cell, one pair being the sex chromosomes. These determine the sex of the individual. In females they are XX, and in males they are XY.

During the first few weeks the foetus develops as a female. However, the Y chromosome contains genes that switch the development of the foetus into the male route. How does this happen? At about six weeks, genes on the Y chromosome cause the reproductive organs in the embryo to develop into testes (the male reproductive organs). Without the action of these genes the organs will develop into ovaries (the female reproductive organs). When the reproductive organs have developed in the foetus they produce hormones, which then take over sexual development.

Hormones

These are the chemicals that affect the development of the internal reproductive structures and the external reproductive organs – the genitals.

The testes in the male foetus produce androgens, the most important of which is testosterone. It is testosterone that controls development of the penis and scrotum, and increases muscle, lung and heart capacity. The ovaries in the female foetus produce oestrogen and progesterone, which lead to the development of the womb and the vagina. In fact, both sexes produce these hormones, but in different quantities.

Summary of the biological differences between males and females

Biological differences	Female	Male
Chromosome pairing	XX	XY
Gonads (the reproductive organs)	Ovaries	Testes
Hormones	More oestrogen and progesterone	More androgens (including testosterone)
Genitalia (external sex organs)	Clitoris and vagina	Penis and scrotum

ASK YOURSELF

Identify the male and female hormones.

ASK YOURSELF

Do you know the difference between sex and gender?

For most individuals all the above features correspond; for instance, a boy will have the XY chromosome pairing, testes, higher levels of androgens, a penis and scrotum. However, sometimes disorders occur; for example, a male foetus may produce testosterone but his body does not respond to it. As a result, male characteristics do not develop.

SEX AND GENDER

The words 'sex' and 'gender' are sometimes used as though they mean the same thing, and on other occasions as though they have different meanings.

Sex refers to the biological aspects of the individual, such as those described above (for example, a child's sex is identified at birth by its genitals) while gender refers to the psychological and cultural aspects of maleness or femaleness (for example, wearing a dress if male may not be regarded as socially acceptable in many cultures).

Sex identity is defined as the biological status of being male or female. As we saw above, in most individuals the four biological indicators of sex, which are listed in the table above, correspond to the individual's sexual identity.

The genitals are the usual indicators of the sex of a newborn infant because they are visible, and it is from this point that the child's development is influenced by its experiences. These experiences contribute to our **gender identity**. Some adults whose sex identity is male say they feel as though they are female; we say their gender identity is female. So, gender identity refers to the individual's feelings of being either male or female. These experiences are linked to the expectations every society has about its members, about what behaviours, characteristics, attitudes, jobs and so on are appropriate for males and for females. These expectations are called **gender roles**.

EXAM STYLE QUESTIONS

Read the following example of a conversation and answer the question:

Colin: 'My son Patrick is acting in quite an aggressive manner towards some of his friends. My daughter Lizzy never did this when she was his age.'
Jack: 'I wouldn't worry, boys normally act like that. It's in their nature.'

Referring to the conversation above, explain the difference between sex identity and gender identity.

Below we examine three explanations of how the developing child comes to adopt the behaviours and attitudes that society sees as appropriate to its sex and how as a result its gender identity develops.

The three theories are:
- The psychodynamic explanation
- The social learning theory
- Gender schema theory.

The psychodynamic explanation

Sigmund Freud developed his psychodynamic theory as a result of his work with patients who suffered paralysis, phobias or extreme anxiety without any apparent physical cause. He was working in the late 1800s in Vienna, using techniques such as hypnosis and dream analysis. From the case studies of his patients, he concluded that their problems were rooted in early experiences in their lives of which they had no memory.

Figure 8.2 Sigmund Freud – known as the father of psychoanalysis

Freud proposed that instinctive drives, such as those required to satisfy hunger or thirst, underlie human behaviour. He labelled this bundle of desires the 'id'; it is buried, along with unpleasant or frightening thoughts, in an inaccessible part of our minds that Freud called the unconscious. He explained the development of our personality and behaviours, including our gender identity, in terms of the way we cope with these desires.

According to psychodynamic theory there are three parts to our personality, which develop as follows:

- The **id**, containing our basic instincts and drives, is present at birth. It is concerned only with immediate satisfaction of these desires; so the baby grabs biscuits that are on a plate. The id works on the pleasure principle ('I want')
- The **ego** starts developing at around three years of age, as we begin to understand that we cannot always have what we want. We begin to find realistic and safe ways of satisfying our desires; so the child may ask if he can have a biscuit. The ego works on the reality principle ('Think about it')
- The **superego** develops at around six years of age and is the moral part of our personality. It is concerned with right and wrong in our behaviour. The superego has two parts: the conscience and the ego-ideal. The superego works on the morality principle ('It is wrong to...').

The ego is in touch with reality: its role is to resolve the conflict between the urgent demands of the selfish id and the restraints of the superego. We are not aware of this conflict because it occurs in the unconscious, but we are aware of the anxiety it creates. The ego must protect itself by finding a way of coping with this anxiety, and Freud proposed a number of ego-defence mechanisms that protect us. These include:

Ego-defence mechanism	Explanation
Displacement	Transferring our negative feelings towards something that will not harm us (for example, shouting at somebody who hasn't done anything, but you are in a bad mood)
Sublimation	Channelling negative energies into an acceptable activity (such as sport as an outlet for aggression)
Identification	Adopting and internalising the ideas and behaviours of another person

Oedipus complex and Electra complex

At about four years of age, one of the life-enhancing drives (the libido) becomes focused on the genitals. According to Freud, this generates a desire for the opposite-sex parent. The child sees the same-sex parent as a rival and wants this parent out of the way. The child also fears that the same-sex parent will be very angry when this desire is discovered. This conflict creates anxiety in the child, which is resolved as follows:

A boy experiences the Oedipus complex because of his desire for his mother and his fear that his father will castrate him. To resolve this conflict (to reduce anxiety), the boy identifies with his father: he adopts his father's behaviours, speech and attitudes. This reduces the threat from his father and, through identification with his father, the boy internalises male characteristics and acquires his male identity.

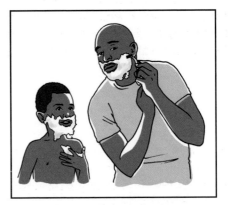

A girl experiences the Electra complex: she has unconscious longings for her father, experiencing penis envy, yet fears the loss of her mother's love. Because she thinks she has already been castrated by her mother, she is not as fearful of her as the boy is of his father. Her identification with her mother, in order to reduce the conflict, is therefore less strong than that of the boy. Nevertheless, she adopts and internalises the characteristics of her mother and so acquires her female identity.

These feelings, and the way they are resolved, all take place in the child's unconscious. Freud called this the phallic stage of psychosexual development, and it is completed by the age of about six years.

KEY STUDY

Freud (1909): Little Hans

Aim: To treat Little Hans's phobia (however, Freud had minimal therapeutic input). A secondary aim was to explore what factors might have led to the phobia in the first place, and what factors led to its remission.

Method: Little Hans was a five-year-old boy whose parents followed Freud's ideas. The boy had been very frightened when he saw a horse fall in the street. He thought it was dead. Subsequently he developed an extreme fear (phobia) of horses; he feared they would bite him and that they would fall down. Over several months the boy's father wrote to Freud, describing incidents and conversations that seemed to be related to his phobia. Hans told his father that he imagined he was given a much larger penis and agreed with his father's suggestion that he wanted to be like his father.

Results/Conclusion: Freud interpreted this information in terms of the Oedipus conflict, noting evidence of the boy's sexual longings for his mother. Freud proposed that the horse represented the child's father, who Hans wished would leave or die. Hans was also frightened that his penis would be cut off; according to Freud, this was linked to his fear of being bitten by the horse.

RESEARCH METHODS

The Little Hans study is an example of a case study. A description of a case study and its advantages and disadvantages can be found in Chapter 10: Research methods and ethics – part 2, pages 180–181.

⚖ **EVALUATION BOX**

Freud's ideas have made a huge impact on psychology, psychiatry and many other areas of life, such as literature and films. This is partly because it offers explanations on so many topics. For example, we refer to psychodynamic ideas in this book under aggression and gender identity.

However, Freud's theory is very controversial. Let's consider some of the criticisms:

- He relied on his patients' memories, which may not have been accurate (this is known as retrospective data)
- He used a few case studies of his female patients, who all came from a similar background, so his sample was not representative of people in general: their behaviour cannot be generalised to other people
- He did not study children directly (for example, the case study of Little Hans involved Freud communicating by letter to Hans's father), yet much of his theory is based on childhood experiences
- Because he uses concepts such as 'libido' and 'identification', which are not directly observable and measurable, it is extremely difficult to test his theory scientifically. If these conflicts are in the unconscious as Freud described, then they are not accessible for studying and testing, as we cannot see them
- Freud's explanation ignores the effect of biological factors (such as genes and hormones) and social influences (as proposed by social learning theory) on gender development.

Freud's theory is very dated and there are several implications of it that need to be considered in today's society. They are as follows:

- There is no evidence that women have weaker gender identity or moral development
- The child must have a parent of each sex for gender identity to develop as Freud described, so children raised in one-parent, lesbian or homosexual families should have difficulties in developing their gender identity. However, several studies have compared children raised in one-parent, two-parent, lesbian and homosexual homes and found no evidence of problems with gender identity
- Children much younger than four years old have some understanding of gender identity, such as preferring gender-typed toys, activities and playmates.

🔑 **KEY TERMS**

Retrospective data – data obtained from a person's memories, for example: 'Think back to when you were a child . . .'

Case study – a detailed study of an individual.

EXAM STYLE QUESTIONS

EXAM STYLE QUESTIONS

Michael is seven years old. He currently wants to be like his father, yet when he was younger, he idolised his mother. How would psychodynamic theory explain Michael's gender development?

The social learning explanation

According to social learning theory, a girl learns what it means to be a girl, and a boy what it means to be a boy, through observation, imitation and reinforcement.

Observation

Children notice what other people do and how they do it, what they say and how they say it. They notice how other people respond to what is said or done, so they observe the consequences of other people's behaviour. As a result of this observation, the child may then imitate, or copy, the behaviour. These are the principles established by Albert Bandura, largely as a result of his research on aggression. You can read more about social learning theory in Chapter 9: Aggression, pages 165–167.

Imitation and models

Anyone whose behaviour is observed is called a model. Bandura found that children are more likely to imitate the behaviour of models that are:

- **Similar** – such as someone of the same sex. The results of Bandura's research on aggression showed that children produced twice as many acts of imitative aggression when they had seen aggression performed by a same-sex model than when an opposite-sex model had performed the aggressive act. They learn what is appropriate for their sex by noting how often behaviour is performed by others of the same sex. This indicates to them what is typical of their own sex, as well as of the other sex. As Bandura noted, when a boy saw a woman kick the Bobo doll, he commented: 'Ladies shouldn't do things like that.'
- **Reinforced** – if the child sees that the model's behaviour leads to pleasant consequences (such as gaining approval) this is called **vicarious reinforcement** because the child is reinforced indirectly. So, a boy who sees a man congratulated for his bravery is more likely to observe and remember his actions.

The child may later imitate the model's behaviour, which may be one reason why children enjoy toys or activities related to their sex. For instance, girls like make-up because they see women using it, and boys like playing football because that is what men do.

ASK YOURSELF

How do you think social learning theory explains how gender identity develops? What factors might affect our gender identity?

ASK YOURSELF

How many times have you seen a little girl copying her mum by putting on make-up, or a little boy copying his dad by having his own tool kit?

ASK YOURSELF

Advertisers use the idea of vicarious reinforcement in the selling of products. Can you think of any examples?

ASK YOURSELF

Can you think of any 'typical' male and female toys? What would happen if a boy was given typical female toys or vice versa?

Figure 8.3 An example of how social learning theory can explain gender development

Look in a toy catalogue and observe the toys dedicated to girls and then those dedicated to boys. Write up your findings. What do your findings show? How does this support the idea that children learn through observation?

Manstead and McCulloch (1981)

Aim: To investigate the role of the media and gender stereotypes.

Method: Antony Manstead and Caroline McCulloch used the **content-analysis technique**. They analysed all advertisements transmitted by a TV channel over seven evenings, except for repeats and those portraying only children or fantasy characters. The total sample was 170. They noted the central figures in terms of various characteristics, such as role, whether they were product users or authorities on the product, and reasons for using the product.

Results: The results showed that 70 per cent of the figures seen to give authoritative information about products were male, but 65 per cent of product users were female; women appeared much more frequently in dependent roles and men in autonomous roles; 64 per cent of figures seen at work were males, whereas 73 per cent of figures seen at home were females; females were more likely to use a product for reasons of social approval or self-enhancement.

Conclusion: Males were more likely to be portrayed as authoritative, workers, independent and active, and females as dependent, home-based, consumers and passive. The advertisements portrayed different roles for males and females that reflected current gender stereotypes. Social learning theory proposes that advertisements such as these provide models of appropriate gender behaviour.

Figure 8.4 A woman driving machinery at a construction site

ACTIVITY

What does figure 8.4 say about how stereotypes are changing? Write down your answer.

Can you think of any stereotypical male and female jobs? Write down three of each.

Have a look at a children's book or children's TV programme and determine whether it displays stereotypical behaviour of males and females. Report your findings in a table.

Terry Frueh and Paul McGhee (1975) investigated the amount of television that primary-school children watched and how stereotypical their ideas of gender were. Their results showed that children who watched a lot of television had fairly stereotypical ideas; those who watched little television had less stereotypical ideas.

ASK YOURSELF

What does this research suggest about the role of the media?

Reinforcement

In accordance with the principles of operant conditioning, if a behaviour is rewarded it is more likely to be repeated. So, if a little girl imitates behaviour she has observed, such as putting on lipstick, and is then told: 'What a pretty lady you are,' she is more likely to repeat the behaviour. If a young boy starts crying and his father says: 'Boys don't cry, only girls do,' he is less likely to repeat the behaviour. Can you think of any other examples of language used by parents/adults when talking to children based on the principles of operant conditioning? Write down your answers.

Beverly Fagot (1978) carried out naturalistic observations of the interactions between parents and their two-year-old children. She found that the girls were rewarded for playing with dolls and helping, whereas boys were rewarded for being independent and active in their play. Parents encouraged boys to climb, but disapproved when their daughters did so. The conclusions are that parents treat sons and daughters differently and encourage them in gender-related activities.

According to the principles of operant conditioning, behaviour that is not appropriate, such as a boy wearing lipstick, will be weakened if it is ignored or frowned upon.

We have seen that social learning theory proposes that the child learns to behave as a male or a female through the processes of:

- Observation of models (such as people who are similar or who are reinforced for their behaviour)
- Imitation of these models if the imitation is followed by positive reinforcement
- Punishment of behaviour that is not in accordance with the child's sex.

Karen Bussey and Albert Bandura (1984) extended these points by proposing that gender-typed behaviour is initially shaped by the responses of others, but as the child gets older he or she begins to note what seems to be appropriate behaviour for each sex. For example, the male child will imitate behaviour associated with males even if it is modelled by a female. These behaviours become internalised and the child can behave in ways it has never seen modelled. In this way the child gradually constructs its own gender identity.

EVALUATION BOX

Social learning theory provides an explanation for the acquisition of gender identity that takes account of the wider social context in which the child lives. It also takes account of

EVALUATION BOX – (continued)

the child's understanding of its world, because cognitive factors such as seeing, remembering and inference are necessary for learning to take place.

As you might expect, there are criticisms and implications of this explanation, and we will look at some of these now. Social learning theory:

- Fails to include biological factors, such as the role of genes or hormones
- Does not account adequately for the consistency in children's behaviour that researchers have identified. As an example, parents who are very careful not to stereotype or promote gender-related behaviour in their children still have children who express stereotypical views and behaviours.

Implications of the social learning explanation

Other weaknesses in this explanation are revealed when we consider some of the implications of the social learning explanation.

Research by Peter LaFreniere and his colleagues (1984) aimed to find out what sex of playmate a child preferred. They observed children up to five years old, noting how often they played with playmates of the same or opposite sex. The results are shown in the following table:

Percentage of children approaching a same-sex child to play with

Age of child	Percentage of approaches to same-sex child
18 months	52%
Three years	62%
Five years	70%

EXAM STYLE QUESTIONS

Using your knowledge of psychology, from the perspective of the social learning approach, explain the development of gender identity.

ACTIVITY

Draw a bar chart to display the information in the table above; be sure to give it an appropriate title and label your axis correctly.

So, what does the LaFreniere *et al.* study show? We can conclude that children prefer same-sex playmates by three years of age. Keeping in mind that adults rarely reinforce children for playing with a same-sex child, it would seem unlikely that this preference is due solely to imitation of same-sex models as social learning would propose.

Also:

- Children reared in one-parent or homosexual families do not have difficulties with the development of gender identity. There is no evidence that the absence of a powerful same-sex model, or the presence of non-stereotypical models for male or female behaviour, affects a child's gender identity
- Children persist in behaviour that is not reinforced. The film *Billy Elliot* is an example of this. Billy was drawn to ballet and desperately wanted to be a ballet dancer, despite being surrounded by stereotypical men who tried to stop him. The only ballet dancers he saw were female. He did not want to be female; he was comfortable as a male. He just wanted to dance.

Figure 8.5 The film *Billy Elliot* demonstrates how children can persist in behaviour that is not reinforced

To summarise, while social learning theory proposes that children's gender identity is created by their environment, we have seen that it is unable to explain all the factors related to gender behaviour in children.

Gender schema theory

The final theory that attempts to explain how gender identity develops is the gender schema theory, put forward by Lawrence Kohlberg in 1966. He suggested that a child develops their gender identity using their cognitive development. He suggested that there were three stages that a child goes through when developing their gender identity.

Stage	Name of stage	Age that it occurs	Description
1	Gender labelling	Up to three years old	By about the age of 18 months a child knows whether it is a boy or a girl ('I am a boy'). By the age of two-and-a-half years, they can identify other children according to their gender ('She is a girl'). However, the child does not know at this age that we stay the same sex throughout our life, and that we stay the same sex even if we change our appearance: for example, if a girl was to put trousers on it doesn't mean that she becomes a boy.
2	Gender stability	Three to five years old	Gender stability occurs when the child realises that their sex is stable and remains unchanged throughout life. For example, a four-year-old boy knows that he will become a man when he grows up. However, a child in this stage would be very confused by a man in a dress.
3	Gender constancy	Six years onwards	When a child has the understanding that gender remains constant in other people as well as themselves, despite changes in appearance, they have reached this stage. The child is now able to conserve (have the understanding that something remains the same even though its appearance changes). Kohlberg suggested that at this stage the child pays more attention to people of the same sex and adopts their behaviours, attitudes and values and, as a result, adopts their gender role.

ACTIVITY

Read each of the three case studies and then complete the matching activity.

Case study	Activity
Joseph, aged two, watched his father dress up ready to play the role of a pantomime dame. He said: 'When I grow up I will be a girl like daddy.'	According to Kohlberg's gender schema theory, which stage of gender identity is Joseph in?
Paul, aged four, watched his father dress up ready to play the role of a pantomime dame. He was very anxious and said: 'You can't wear that dress, Daddy, dresses are for girls.'	According to Kohlberg's gender schema theory, which stage of gender identity is Paul in?
Pamela, aged nine, watched her mother putting on a suit and tie ready to go to a fancy-dress party as a banker. Pamela laughed and said: 'Mum, you're not much like a man – your voice is too soft.'	According to Kohlberg's gender schema theory, which stage of gender identity is Pamela in?

Figure 8.6 This would be confusing for a child in the gender stability stage

EVALUATION BOX

This theory explains why children, after the age of six, pay more attention to people of the same sex and seek out gender-typed activities. However, it cannot account for the two-year-old's strong preference for toys, friends and activities that are gender related, because at this age children still think that they could grow up to be somebody of the opposite sex.

EXAM STYLE QUESTIONS

The table below contains examples of gender development. For each one identify the correct term from the list below the table and say why it is an example of that.

Behaviour	Term/example of gender development
Linda has just received a new doll and pram for her birthday. She copies her mother pushing her little sister in her pram.	
Stacey sees her favourite character on TV being praised for helping a relative. Stacey is very helpful when her granny visits.	

Choose from the following list:
- Oedipus complex
- Electra complex
- Vicarious reinforcement
- Gender schema
- Imitation
- Modelling

ACTIVITY

Read the following case studies and explain the behaviour of the people in them using the psychodynamic explanation, social learning theory and gender schema theory.

Case study	Psychodynamic explanation	Social learning theory	Gender schema theory
Adam, aged five, wants to be a train driver like his father.			
Sandra, aged four, enjoys pushing her baby doll around in its pram.			
Nigel, aged four, is a page boy at a wedding but he refuses to wear a kilt.			
Minnie, aged five, usually plays with girls at school; she hardly ever plays with boys.			
It is Mike's sixth birthday and he is given a Barbie doll in a pink dress. He bursts into tears and gives it straight to his sister, saying he isn't a girl.			

TEST YOURSELF

1 Explain the difference between the terms sex and gender.
2 Name three biological differences between males and females.
3 What are the three parts of the personality, according to Freud?
4 What is the difference between the Oedipus complex and the Electra complex?
5 What are the three important factors according to social learning theory?
6 Name one piece of research that supports the idea that children develop their gender according to learning through observation.
7 What are the three stages identified by Kohlberg in his theory of gender development?

Aggression

WHAT YOU NEED TO KNOW FOR THE EXAMINATION

What you need to know for the examination:

- Explanations of aggression:
  - Biological, including the role of hormones, brain disease and chromosomal abnormality
  - Psychodynamic, including the frustration-aggression hypothesis
  - Social learning, including modelling, punishment and monitoring

- Description and evaluation of studies of the development of aggressive behaviour
- Ways of reducing aggression based on these explanations
- Evaluation of these ways of reducing aggression

ACTIVITY

Imagine you are writing a dictionary for GCSE psychology students. How could you explain aggression?

Now read the following examples and state whether you think they are aggressive acts or not:

- A woman shouts at her boyfriend in the street for looking at another woman
- A soldier shoots an enemy dead
- A driver gesticulates at another on the motorway for pulling out in front of her
- A young boy spits on another as he walks past
- A man pushes his wife because she gets in his way.

In this chapter we will focus on the kind of aggression that is intentional and destructive. What causes this behaviour? What role do parents play? How can aggression be reduced?

EXPLANATIONS FOR AGGRESSION

EXAM STYLE QUESTIONS

Define what is meant by the term aggression.

ACTIVITY

Do you think that people are born with an aggressive manner, or do they learn it as a result of their environment?

Aggression can be verbal as well as physical. We will begin by considering a variety of explanations that, as you will see, reflect different ways of explaining human behaviour. We will then review some possible ways of reducing aggression based on the three explanations that we will cover. Psychology can provide some useful answers for why people are aggressive and also ways that can help people to reduce their aggressive behaviour.

ACTIVITY

In pairs, brainstorm what you think makes a person aggressive. Try to think of four or five different explanations.

> **KEY TERM**
>
> **Aggression** – antisocial behaviour; generally considered to be behaviour that harms, or intends to harm, someone or something.

Figure 9.1 There are many explanations for why people behave aggressively

ACTIVITY

As a class, prepare a debate considering the following issues:

- Do you think a person's biology can make them aggressive?
- Does this mean that they can't control their aggression?
- Does this mean that people who kill others have something wrong with their brain?

Half of the class needs to argue for the idea that aggression can be explained in a biological way, and the other half need to argue for the role of the environment.

Biological explanation of aggression

The main focus of this approach is that aggression is innate (inborn).

From a biological perspective, researchers have looked at the role of the brain, hormones and chemicals in aggression. They believe that these are important factors in our biology that can affect our behaviour.

The limbic system, which is part of the central nervous system, is linked to aggression. For example, in some animals damage to the limbic system increases aggression and decreases fear. However, damage to the amygdala, which is part of the limbic system, results in timidity.

Research on human brains has been restricted to people with very severe problems requiring brain surgery, although more recent developments in brain scanning have considerably extended the possibilities for research.

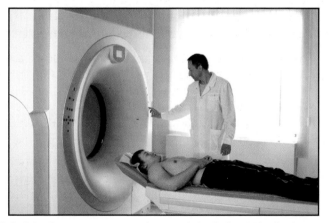

Figure 9.2 A brain scan can reveal a great deal about the brain

The case of Charles Whitman provides an example of how brain damage may cause aggression. Charles Whitman shot his mother, his wife and then more than a dozen students at the University of Texas in 1966 before being killed by police. Prior to this he had asked for help to deal with the overwhelming violent impulses he was experiencing and asked that an autopsy (an examination of the body when a person has died) be performed on him after his death to see if there was any physical disorder. The autopsy revealed a tumour that may have been pressing against his amygdala.

ACTIVITY

How does the example of Charles Whitman support the idea that aggression could be due to a person's biology? Can Charles Whitman be held responsible for his behaviour? Write down your answers.

Psychosurgery (deliberate surgical damage to parts of the brain) to the amygdala has been reported as successfully reducing violent behaviour in other patients, but it may affect other functions as well. Damage to the amygdala may affect a person's ability to read emotional cues (such as facial expressions or tone of voice: see Chapter 2: Non-verbal communication, pages 31–33) or to understand dangerous situations.

The biological approach also indicates that higher levels of certain chemicals or hormones are linked to aggression. For example, the higher level of aggression generally shown by males is associated with their higher levels of testosterone. Research has shown that violent criminals show higher levels of testosterone than non-violent criminals. But higher levels of testosterone have also been found in dominant but non-violent criminals. This suggests that the relationship between aggression and testosterone is complex.

Serotonin has also been linked to aggression; this could be associated with its influence on the reticular activating system (RAS). This RAS keeps us alert to sensory information but serotonin dampens down this effect. Research suggests that lower levels of serotonin are related to higher levels of aggression, perhaps allowing the RAS to be too responsive.

This brief survey suggests several different biological explanations for aggressive behaviour. However, critics argue that the biological explanation fails to take account of how cognitive and social factors may also affect human aggression.

EXAM STYLE QUESTIONS

Read the following case study and explain Peter's behaviour from a biological viewpoint:

Peter is an aggressive young man. He frequently has violent outbursts where he damages property and verbally abuses his neighbours. He claims that he was born like this.

Chromosomal abnormalities

In addition to brain disease and hormone imbalance, some people believe that we may be born with the tendency to be aggressive.

A chromosome is a long, thin strand of DNA found in our cells that carries all of the genetic material that makes us who we are. Humans have 23 pairs of chromosomes in each cell (46 in total), half of which we inherit from our mothers and half from our fathers. The 23rd pair, for instance, determines whether we are male or female.

If one of these pairs is damaged in any way, or if we have more chromosomes than normal, we may show certain physical problems or may suffer with certain psychological problems. Some chromosomal abnormalities occur spontaneously; others may occur if the mother drinks or smokes while pregnant, for instance.

It used to be believed that damage to certain pairings of chromosomes may result in the person being aggressive, for example XYY syndrome. In this there is an extra Y chromosome in the 23rd pair. Research in the 1960s suggested that these people were male, extremely tall and aggressive, bur we have now concluded that this is not the case. The original research was misleading: they are indeed tall and male, but they are not aggressive.

It may be that men with the XYY syndrome have a difficult time during adolescence because of the other effects of the syndrome (there is a high incidence of severe acne, which may result in bullying; there is also a high incidence of learning difficulties and delayed language development; also their height can cause skeletal and movement problems), so some may suffer with behavioural problems later in life. This is not to say that the chromosomal abnormality itself causes the behavioural problems; if anything, the behavioural problems are a side effect of the chromosomal abnormality.

While it is true that chromosome damage can influence the way we look and behave, and the development of our brain, there is very little evidence to suggest that chromosome abnormalities are responsible for aggressive behaviour.

Psychodynamic explanation of aggression

The main focus of this approach is that aggression is innate (inborn). One of the explanations put forward from this approach is the frustration-aggression hypothesis.

The frustration-aggression hypothesis

John Dollard and his associates (1939) proposed that aggression is caused by frustration, and therefore that anyone who is frustrated will behave aggressively. This became known as the frustration-aggression hypothesis, which proposes that people are motivated to reach goals but, if they are blocked, then frustration occurs. For example, if a task is too difficult or someone stops us from doing something we will become frustrated and then, because we are frustrated, we behave aggressively.

ACTIVITY

Can you think of an occasion when you were frustrated? Did it result in you behaving aggressively?

This explanation argues that aggression may be delayed or directed onto a target other than the cause of the frustration. An example of this is scapegoating, when aggression is turned onto an individual or group that is not the cause of frustration but is a 'safe target', because it is less powerful and not likely to retaliate.

ACTIVITY

Read the following scenario and identify the scapegoat:

Nicholas has had a bad day at work. He was supposed to meet his target of selling a certain number of ice creams but it has been raining all day and people haven't been to the beach where he parks his van. On his way home the car in front of him is driving very slowly; Nicholas beeps his horn and shouts at the driver as he overtakes.

However, some studies have shown that aggression is raised only slightly when participants are frustrated. Neal Miller (1941) identified several reasons why an individual might not show aggressive behaviour:

- They might think it is wrong to behave aggressively

- They might have learned not to show aggression
- They might be frightened that the other person would be aggressive towards them
- They might think that although the other person made them frustrated, it was not done intentionally.

Accordingly, the hypothesis was modified to state that frustration *may* cause aggression.

So, aggression is not always shown; whether it is or not depends on the individual's past experiences, the other people involved in the situation and its meaning for the individual. In addition, frustration may lead to other consequences, such as apathy or hopelessness.

The notion of frustration was taken up by Leonard Berkowitz (1968) who argued that frustration does not cause aggression directly, but does arouse anger. The anger in turn creates a readiness to act aggressively. If there are aggressive cues in the environment – a gun, for example – this makes the individual more likely to be aggressive.

KEY STUDY

Berkowitz (1968)

Aim: To investigate the idea that people could learn to associate a particular stimulus (such as a gun) with anger or ways of releasing anger.

Method: Berkowitz demonstrated this in a series of experiments in which participants were angered by someone who was a confederate in the experiment. Participants were then given the opportunity to deliver mild shocks to the confederate. Some participants saw a shotgun and revolver next to the shock switches, and some of these participants were told they belonged to the person who had made them angry. Another group saw neutral objects such as a badminton racket, and a control group saw no other objects.

Results: The results showed that more shocks were delivered by participants who saw the guns than those in the groups that saw a badminton racket or no objects.

Conclusion: Berkowitz proposed that people learn to associate particular stimuli (such as a gun, a boxing match, or a person) with anger or ways of releasing anger. When the individual is frustrated this creates anger and a gun, for example, becomes a cue for aggression.

RESEARCH METHODS

Berkowitz's study is an example of a laboratory experiment. A description of a laboratory experiment and is advantages and disadvantages can be found in Chapter 5: Research methods and ethics – part 1, pages 70–71.

This explanation for aggression is linked to the principles of classical conditioning and, like Robert Baron's research described later in the chapter, on page 172, it stresses the role of situational cues in determining whether aggression occurs.

The social learning explanation of aggression

The main focus of this approach is that aggression is learned behaviour.

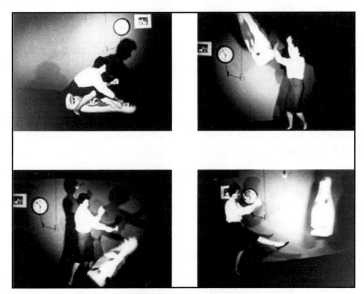

Figure 9.3 The Bobo doll study by Bandura: a famous investigation into aggression

According to social learning principles, children learn aggression by:

- Observation of others: those who are observed are called models; models are likely to be people the child sees as similar to themselves or as being more powerful, or who are rewarded for their aggression
- Imitation of the model's behaviour
- Reinforcement when the child imitates the behaviour.

The type of research that led to these conclusions was conducted by Albert Bandura.

⊕ KEY STUDY

Bandura *et al.* (1961)

Aim: To test the idea that children could learn to become aggressive through imitating another person behaving aggressively.

Method: In Bandura's basic procedure, children aged between three and five years old saw an adult behave aggressively towards a large inflatable doll (called a Bobo doll).

Figure 9.4 These photographs were taken during Bandura's experiments

Results: They then had the chance to play with a range of toys, including a Bobo doll, while observers watched their behaviour. One of the findings was that the children showed significantly more imitation of a same-sex model, and boys performed more acts of aggression than girls, as the following table shows:

KEY STUDY – (continued)

Mean scores of imitative aggression of a male and a female model

Participant's gender	Female model	Male model
Female	19	9
Male	17	38

In variations on this procedure, Bandura and his colleagues divided the participants into three groups, each seeing a different consequence after the model's aggression. The observations showed that seeing a model punished resulted in the lowest levels of imitative behaviour, which is an example of vicarious (not direct) punishment. In contrast, highest levels of aggression were produced in children who saw the model praised (vicarious reinforcement), but children seeing no consequences for the model also showed high levels of aggression.

This research also provided evidence that children knew what behaviour was appropriate for the models, because some of them commented that 'ladies shouldn't do things like that'.

When the children were asked to reproduce as much of the model's behaviour as they could remember (and were rewarded for doing this), all of them were able to reproduce most of the aggressive acts. This was true even with children who had seen the model punished (which had resulted in the lowest level of imitation).

Conclusion: We can conclude that all the children had learned the behaviour, but they were more likely to imitate same-sex or reinforced models.

ACTIVITY

Draw a bar chart to display the information above. Be sure to give it an appropriate title and label your axis correctly.

ACTIVITY

Describe one example of real-life aggressive behaviour and apply social learning theory to explain why the aggression occurred. Write down your answers.

Reinforcement is an important explanation for why children might persist in these imitative acts. This is what Gerald Patterson and his colleagues (1967) found in their observational study of young children.

KEY STUDY

Patterson *et al.* (1967)

Aim: To investigate the effects of negative reinforcement on aggressive behaviour.

Method: Children were watched in an observational study.

Results: The researchers noted acts of interpersonal aggression and the immediate consequences of the actions. Results showed that, for children showing the highest levels of aggression, the most common consequence was a rewarding one for the child.

Children who were aggressive and were then punished (the victim fought back) were the least likely to be aggressive. However, Patterson found evidence of negative reinforcement in children who were not very aggressive. If they sometimes fought back when they were attacked, they gradually became more aggressive themselves.

Conclusion: Overall these results suggest that if aggressive behaviour is reinforced, it is more likely to be repeated.

RESEARCH METHODS

Patterson's study is an example of an observation. A description of an observation and its advantages and disadvantages can be found in Chapter 10: Research methods and ethics – part 2, pages 179–180.

EXAM STYLE QUESTIONS

Describe and evaluate one study in which aggression was investigated. Include in your answer the method used, the results, the conclusion and, in your evaluation, one strength and one weakness of the study.

Reinforcement also explains why aggressive behaviour might take place in one situation but not in another. For example, a child might learn that his teacher disapproves when he acts out a violent scene from a film he has watched, so he no longer performs it in front of the teacher. But this behaviour wins admiration from his peers, so he does it in the playground, out of the teacher's sight.

ACTIVITY

Do you think that social learning theory suggests that the media have an effect on aggression? You will have heard of cases where people have injured others and said that they were imitating a character in a particular film. Do you think this could be true? Suggest arguments for and against.

Critics of the social learning approach assert that it overemphasises the influence of the environment and experience, and underestimates the importance of inherited or biological factors. Also, that it does not put enough emphasis on the human ability to reason or consider moral issues. if it were completely true that the media could reinforce aggression in people imitating a particular film/character, then everybody would imitate the behaviour and engage in antisocial behaviour.

Critics of laboratory experiments of aggression question whether the results can be generalised to everyday life: in the laboratory experiments of Berkowitz and Bandura the variables are controlled and it is likely that behaviour will not be realistic. More naturalistic methods, such as Patterson's observations of children, show the complexity of human aggression; as the children were unaware that they were being watched, variables wouldn't have been controlled and the behaviour is more likely to be natural.

EXAM STYLE QUESTIONS

Read the following explanations of aggression and identify the explanation from either the biological perspective, psychodynamic perspective, or the social learning perspective.

Explanation of aggression	Psychological perspective
Susan has observed and imitated the behaviour of her best friend, who is very aggressive.	
John has very high levels of testosterone, which experts believe make him aggressive.	
Alan becomes frustrated easily, which leads him to behave in an aggressive manner.	

WAYS OF REDUCING AGGRESSION

One of the reasons for studying aggression is to identify ways in which it may be reduced. We will study methods based on the explanations we have considered.

The biological approach

The biological approach would suggest that aggression could be reduced through the use of surgery or chemicals in the form of drugs. As we have mentioned, surgery on the amygdala has reduced aggressive behaviour in very violent people, while castration has been found to reduce aggressive behaviour in very violent men. Psychosurgery is a complex and extreme form of treatment, and both psychosurgery and castration raise many ethical concerns.

Although biological methods may be successful in reducing aggression, they are very drastic and raise major ethical concerns. Also, because we do not fully understand which parts of the brain and what processes are involved in aggression, it is difficult to devise treatments for specific problems.

Aggression may be reduced by drugs that slow down or lower the body's response to stimuli, but these drugs may also cause drowsiness, inability to concentrate, loss of memory, loss of appetite and so on. This in turn may lead to the person losing their job, poor health or deterioration in social relationships, which may be more damaging than the original condition.

The psychodynamic approach

Sport provides an opportunity for sublimation: channelling aggression into acceptable activities. But Freud also argued that simply watching competitive sport was cathartic: it released pent-up aggression.

Figure 9.5 Watching sport is believed to be a way of reducing aggression

Freud also argued that the displacement of aggression prevents us from destroying ourselves. This involves transferring aggression outwards and onto someone or something else (a defence mechanism). To avoid aggression against others, this aggression should be directed at objects: punching a cushion, throwing a soft ball at the wall or digging vigorously in the garden should all release aggression.

According to Berkowitz, frustration is more likely to lead to aggression if there is an aggressive cue present.

🧩 KEY STUDY

Baron (1977)

Aim: To test whether there were certain factors that could reduce aggression.

Method: In a field experiment Robert Baron arranged for a car to break down at traffic lights when there was a male driver in the car behind. While the blocked-in driver was waiting, a woman crossed the road in front of him. The woman wore either a revealing dress, a clown's costume, used crutches or wore normal clothes.

To measure the levels of aggression shown by the drivers, the observers rated them on measures such as amount of bad language used, honking their horns and hostile gestures.

Results: Results showed that in the first three conditions drivers showed lower levels of aggression than when the woman was dressed normally or when no woman crossed.

Conclusion: Baron concluded that aggression can be reduced by sexual arousal, humour or empathy, perhaps because these are emotions that are incompatible with anger.

🔍 RESEARCH METHODS

Baron's study is an example of a field experiment. A description of a field experiment and its advantages and disadvantages can be found in Chapter 5: Research methods and ethics – part 1, pages 71–72.

✏️ ACTIVITY

An observation is an excellent way to gather qualitative data about human behaviour. Conduct an observation on either (or both if possible):

• The behaviour of drivers at traffic lights
• The behaviour of football fans at a school match.

Your task is to count the number of aggressive acts that you observe.

When you have completed the observation, outline one strength and one weakness of using observations to collect data on your chosen behaviour (football fans or drivers). Discuss your answers with other people in your class.

There is little evidence that Freud's proposals do reduce aggression. Research in a laboratory setting that studied displacement suggests the opposite effect. When participants were given the chance to shock another person who could not retaliate, participants gave higher levels of shock. Leonard Berkowitz (1968) found that participants who were angry became even more punitive, whereas Freud would predict that they would become less punitive as their aggression was released.

Other research contradicts the benefits of sport on aggression. R. Arms and colleagues (1979) compared the effects of watching high-contact sports (wrestling and ice hockey) with a swimming event. Participants watching wrestling and ice hockey experienced increased feelings of hostility, whereas those watching swimming did not. We can conclude that watching competitive sport is not necessarily cathartic; indeed it may lead to increased aggression for spectators of high-contact sports.

Nevertheless, it seems that aggression may be reduced by directing it towards a 'safe' object or by the use of non-aggressive cues. People can be taught how to use these techniques to manage their anger and aggression.

The social learning approach

According to social learning theory, and Bandura's research, if we see models punished for aggressive behaviour we should be less likely to show aggression. But seeing non-aggressive models can also reduce aggression. Baron (1977) gave participants the opportunity to give electric shocks to someone. In fact this person was a confederate who pretended to be receiving the shocks. The experimental group of participants had previously seen a non-aggressive model; the control group had not seen a model. Baron found that those seeing a non-aggressive model gave fewer shocks than those seeing no model. This suggests that seeing non-aggressive models can reduce aggression.

EVALUATION BOX

The role of punishment is a complex one in reducing aggression. An adult who uses an aggressive method of punishing the child (such as hitting) is modelling aggressive behaviour, showing what to do to get your own way, so the child may later imitate this behaviour.

Aggressive models cannot be totally removed from society. The media have frequently been blamed for providing models for aggressive behaviour, but they also provide non-aggressive models. John Murray (1980) investigated the behaviour of children after watching some programmes on American TV (for example, Sesame Street) that promoted helpfulness and sharing. Results showed that the children's helpful and sharing behaviour increased.

It seems that social learning can be successful in reducing aggression, although some people will still choose mainly aggressive models to imitate.

EXAM STYLE QUESTIONS

Using your knowledge of psychology, describe and evaluate one way of reducing aggressive behaviour.

TEST YOURSELF

1 What do psychologists mean by the term aggression?
2 Which part of the brain is believed to play a part in aggression?
3 Which hormone is said to be excessive in aggressive males?
4 What is the difference between frustration and aggression?
5 How can social learning theory explain how the media may promote aggressive behaviour?
6 How can the biological theory of aggression be applied to reducing aggressive behaviour?
7 How can the frustration-aggression hypothesis be applied to reducing aggressive behaviour?
8 How can the social learning theory be applied to reducing aggressive behaviour?

9 Complete the following table:

Explanations of aggressive behaviour

	Biological explanation	Psychodynamic explanation	Social learning explanation
Description			
Treatment			
Advantage of treatment			
Disadvantage of treatment			

Research methods and ethics – part 2

In addition to the material covered in Chapter 5: Research methods and ethics part 1, if you are studying the full course this is what you need to know for the examination:

Methods of investigation:

- Procedures for non-experimental methods of investigation:
  - ○ Survey methods: questionnaires (including open and closed questions) and interviews (including structured and unstructured)
  - ○ Observation, including categories of behaviour and inter-observational reliability

  - ○ Case studies
- Advantages and disadvantages of these methods of investigation (including ecological validity)

Methods of control, data analysis and data presentation:

- Correlation, including an understanding of association between two variables, and of correlation relationship; advantages and disadvantages of using correlation
- Graphical representations, including scatter graphs

METHODS OF INVESTIGATION

Different methods can be used to investigate behaviour. The non-experimental method is still a scientific method (as the information can be measured) and it can aim for objectivity (as it is fact based).

Survey methods

A survey asks people questions, either through face-to-face interviews or written questionnaires. The questions must be prepared carefully so that they are clear and do not persuade the respondents (the people answering the questions) to answer in a particular way.

The researcher might first conduct a pilot study (a trial) with the questions, giving them to a few people and asking for comments. If the questions are unclear or produce biased answers, the researcher can adjust them for the main study.

There are different ways to conduct a survey: researchers can use a questionnaire or an interview.

Questionnaires

A questionnaire is a good way to gain a great deal of data with a significant number of participants. A questionnaire is a set of questions that are designed to investigate a particular topic. For example, if we wanted to investigate the shopping habits of women we could ask the following questions:

1 Do you enjoy shopping for yourself? YES/NO
2 How many times a month do you go shopping? ONCE/TWICE/ THREE TIMES/MORE
3 Do you shop alone or with a friend or family member? ALONE/WITH A FRIEND

The questions may be closed or open-ended depending on the kind of information the researcher wants:

- **Closed questions** produce clear-cut answers that are easy to interpret and quantify, such as: 'Is your child happy at school? Yes/No?' Respondents may want to answer 'Well, it depends ...' but, because they are forced to choose yes or no, their answer will not reflect their real opinions. A compromise is a question that provides a range of answers, perhaps using a scale from one to five to reflect the strength or amount of agreement. This provides more detailed information that is still easy to quantify
- **Open questions** give the respondent the opportunity to provide a lot of information. They are useful for in-depth research (for example: 'What do you think of your child's school?'); however, it is difficult to compare different people's answers, so the open-ended question is less useful.

Because questionnaires require written answers, they depend on respondents being able to read and understand correctly. They may be distributed by hand, by post or from a distribution point such as a doctor's surgery or supermarket. They can be returned by post or collected by hand once completed. The researcher has no control over how accurately or thoughtfully people answer the questions, whether they understand them correctly or, indeed, whether they return the questionnaires at all.

Questions can be closed or open-ended but must be clear and understandable. Respondents should remain anonymous, so they must not be asked to give their names.

Strengths and weaknesses of questionnaires

Strengths	Weaknesses
• Quick and easy to operate if they use closed questions. • A very large sample can be used, which generates a lot of information. • People who are geographically distant can be studied.	• The sample will be biased because it relies on people returning the questionnaires (they may be returned in greater numbers by people who have plenty of time or strong feelings about the topic). • Respondents may not give accurate answers, perhaps because of misunderstanding of the questions or because of boredom.

Interviews

Another way of conducting a survey is to use an interview. Here the researcher asks the questions face to face. The structure of the interview can vary:

- **Structured interviews** consist of a series of fixed questions with a limited range of possible answers, much like a questionnaire. They are the fastest to complete and, if well prepared, they provide data that are easy to quantify and analyse. However, they do suffer the drawbacks of closed questions. It's the sort of thing you find people doing with clipboards in town on a Saturday afternoon: 'Excuse me, sir, have you got a minute for a short interview?' Does this sound familiar? Look out for this sort of thing next time you are in a busy place!
- **Semi-structured** interviews comprise open-ended questions that cover the information the researcher wants to gain. However, respondents may provide this information without being asked a specific question, so the researcher is flexible about the questions themselves and the order in which they are asked. This style is useful for gaining more in-depth and accurate information from respondents, but it is more difficult to compare answers.

Strengths and weaknesses of interviews

Strengths	Weaknesses
• Detailed information can be obtained. • It avoids oversimplifying complex issues. • Greater attention to an individual's point of view is important in clinical psychology.	• Asking questions face to face may encourage people to give the kind of answers they think the interviewer wants or to give socially desirable answers. • They can be difficult to analyse if unstructured and qualitative in nature. • They can be time-consuming and expensive.

Observations

When psychologists observe, they watch people's behaviour and measure particular aspects in a way that is as precise as possible.

It is usual to have more than one observer because behaviour is complex and the observer may be biased. If the behaviour is videoed, the observers will analyse the behaviour from the video. They need to be trained in how to analyse and measure the behaviour being studied so that they all interpret it in the same way. When they can interpret the data in the same way we say that there is inter-observer reliability.

Behaviour is noted on an observation schedule. The researchers must decide what behaviours are to be noted. This is quite complex. For instance, measures of aggression might include pushing, kicking, various facial expressions and shouting.

Decisions must be made about how the participants will be observed and over what time period. Observers may watch a child for a full playgroup session or they may observe a child for five minutes every 15 minutes. This is called time sampling.

If they are interested in behaviour in a particular setting, they will observe the participants in that setting, such as any child who comes to play in the sand box.

The behaviour may be analysed by being broken down into behaviour categories. Here the observer would note each time a child performed one of these behaviours. The observer may have categories of behaviour on the schedule, such as playing alone, playing with one other, playing in a group or interacting with an adult. The task here would be to categorise the behaviour and note how much time is spent performing that particular behaviour.

Strengths and weaknesses of observations

Strengths	Weaknesses
• If the people do not know that they are being observed they will display more natural behaviour, and hence increase the ecological validity of the investigation. • It is a good way to observe people in their natural environment.	• If the people do not know that they are being observed, then they will not be able to give consent to take part. This raises ethical concerns.

Case studies

The case study is an in-depth study of one person or a small number of people.

It may include interviews (using open-ended questions) of the person being studied, as well as others who can provide information about the person's past or present experiences and behaviours. Data provided by school or medical records may also be gathered. Because of the detail they provide, they may suggest insights to the psychologist and ideas for further work.

For example, a case study may be written about a child who is having trouble in school. Teachers may be interviewed, as may the family of the child and the child itself. The researchers may obtain the child's medical records and they may observe the child in school and at home. A case study would then be written using all of this information.

Freud used case studies of his patients to devise and generate his theories (see Key Study on Little Hans on page 145).

Strengths and weaknesses of case studies

Strengths	Weaknesses
• Gives a detailed picture of the individual. • It can be useful in treating individual problems and, by studying those who are unusual, psychologists can discover more about what is usual. • Although the information gained about one person cannot be generalised to others, the case study can form the basis for future research.	• Records may be inaccurate or incomplete. • The interviewer may be biased towards what they expect to find. • The findings of case studies cannot be generalised to others.

METHODS OF CONTROL, DATA ANALYSIS AND DATA PRESENTATION

Correlational study

Sometimes psychologists want to find out which behaviours go together, for example to see whether the amount of violent television watched is related to the amount of aggression shown. Both the variables may already be occurring but, in order to find out if they are related, the psychologist must measure the variables and then calculate a correlation.

There are two patterns of correlation:

- A **positive correlation** occurs when one variable increases as the other increases; for example, as the temperature increases so does the number of ice creams sold
- A **negative correlation** occurs when one variable increases as the other decreases; for example, as the temperature drops, the number of jumpers sold increases.

It is important to remember that a correlational study can only show a relationship between two variables; we cannot assume that one variable causes the other.

For example, there might be a positive relationship between sightings of storks and number of babies born: there is an increase in the birth rate around springtime, and there is an increase in stork sightings around then too, but storks do not bring babies! In this case one variable does not cause the other.

Correlations are a way of gaining more information about variables that cannot be controlled, and enable us to predict the value of one variable from the other one. They can be used when it would be unethical to conduct an experiment (for example, to see whether there is a correlation between the security of a child's attachment and their level of disobedience) and may form the basis for a follow-up study to test cause and effect.

Graphical representations

Scatter graphs

A scatter graph is used to display a correlation between two variables. A scatter graph will either show a positive correlation (meaning that there is a positive relationship between the two variables), a negative correlation (meaning that there is a negative relationship between the two variables) or no correlation (meaning that there is no relationship at all between the two variables).

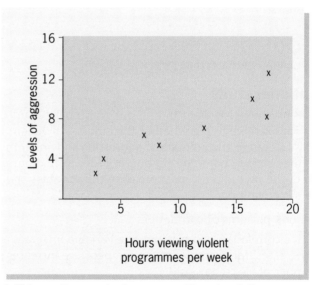

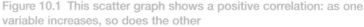

Figure 10.1 This scatter graph shows a positive correlation: as one variable increases, so does the other

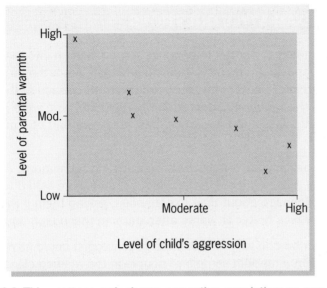

Figure 10.2 This scatter graph shows a negative correlation: as one variable increases, the other decreases

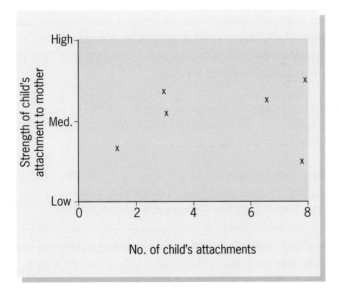

Figure 10.3 This scatter graph shows no correlation

EXAM STYLE QUESTIONS

A psychologist wanted to conduct some research into the effectiveness of a memory-training exercise. From the target population of people who frequently went to classes at the local library, she randomly selected ten participants who were part of a reading class and ten participants who were part of a maths class.

Both classes were taught memory-boosting techniques. After a week of teaching them the techniques, they were asked to fill in a questionnaire about their experiences, asking them if their memory was better or worse after learning these techniques.

1 Describe one way in which the psychologist could have chosen a random sample of people in the reading class.
2 Questionnaires cannot be used to gather information from a large group of people. True or false?
3 Identify one disadvantage of using a questionnaire in psychological research.
4 The psychologist then wanted to carry out a case study on one of the participants who reported a massive increase in her memory. Outline what is meant by a case study.
5 The results from the two groups who took part in the memory-boosting classes are as follows:

	Percentage of respondents
Memory had improved	70%
Memory had got worse	2%
Memory had stayed the same	28%

Draw a bar chart to display the percentages shown; provide a suitable title for this bar chart and fully label your axis.
6 Write one open question that the psychologist could have used in her questionnaire.
7 Write one closed question that the psychologist could have used in her questionnaire.

GLOSSARY

altruism   behaviour that puts someone's well-being before your own, perhaps in a way that is damaging to yourself, without thought of reward

audience effects   the effects that the presence of others has on the performance of a task

bystander intervention   the way in which people who witness an incident behave

case study   a detailed study of an individual's (or a small group's) background

categorisation   grouping things together on the basis of some similarity

child-rearing style   the way parents bring up children

classical conditioning   a form of learning in which an automatic response becomes associated with a previously unrelated stimulus

conditioned response   the response that occurs when the conditioned stimulus is presented

conditioned stimulus   the stimulus that causes the conditioned response

conditions   the different experiences that groups of participants undergo

confederate   someone who appears to be a participant but who is actually part of the study

cognition/cognitive   anything to do with mental processes such as remembering or thinking

conformity   yielding to real or imagined group pressure

conscience   the part of the superego which stops us from doing things we know to be wrong (Freud)

control condition/control group   the group of participants who do not experience the independent variable

counterbalancing   giving half the participants the experimental condition first and the other participants the control condition first

correlation   a relationship between two variables

correlational study   a study to discover if there is a relationship between two variables

cross-cultural research   research that compares people from different cultures

debriefing   giving a general explanation of the study to participants when they have finished, and ensuring their well-being

deindividuation   a state in which the individual becomes less aware of themselves and has less sense of personal responsibility for their own behaviour

demand characteristics   the clues in an experiment that lead participants to think they know what the researcher is looking for

dependent variable   the outcome of manipulation of the independent variable; the results

diffusion of responsibility   the more bystanders that witness an incident, the less likely it is that one of them will help

discrimination   treating people unfavourably on the basis of their membership of a particular group

ecological validity   the degree to which an investigation represents real-life experiences

ego   the part of personality in touch with reality (Freud)

ego ideal   the part of the superego that represents what we would like to be (Freud)

empathy   the ability to match one's own feelings with those of another person

ethics   desirable standards of behaviour towards others

experiment   a research method in which all variables are controlled except one, so that the effect of that variable can be measured

experimental condition/experimental group   the group of participants who experience the independent variable

extinction when a response to a stimulus is no longer seen

field experiment an experiment that takes place in an everyday environment

frustration–aggression hypothesis the proposal that frustration always leads to aggression

gender the psychological or cultural aspects of maleness or femaleness

gender identity the individual's understanding of what it means to be male or female

generalise to apply information from one situation to other situations

hypothesis a prediction of what will happen

identification the process by which the child comes to take on the ideas and behaviours of the same-sex parent (Freud)

impression formation making inferences about people on the basis of little information

imitation copying the behaviour of a model (social learning theory)

independent groups an experimental design that has different participants in each group

independent variable what the researcher manipulates

in-group/out-group the division of people into two groups: the in-group is the group to which we belong, the out-group is the others

internalise to feel that a behaviour or idea is part of us, that we own it

interview to ask participants questions in a face-to-face setting

learning a relatively permanent change in behaviour that is due to experience

libido the life instinct (Freud)

matched pairs an experimental design in which each group has different participants, but they are paired on the basis of their similarity in several characteristics

model someone whose behaviour the individual imitates (social learning theory)

naive not aware of the real purpose of an experiment or investigation

negative correlation a relationship between two variables in which one increases as the other decreases

negative reinforcement anything that strengthens behaviour because it stops an unpleasant experience

norms the beliefs or expectations that members of a group share

obedience following the orders of someone else, who may be perceived to be in authority

observation research that involves watching and recording behaviour

operant conditioning learning that occurs as a result of reward or punishment

opportunity sampling selecting whomever is available to be a participant

out-group homogeneity seeing members of the out-group as more similar to one another than they are

peripheral traits personality traits that are affected by central traits

phallic stage the stage of psychosexual development when the libido is focused on the genitals and the Oedipus or Electra conflict occurs (Freud)

pluralistic ignorance when each bystander takes no action and thus misleads the others into defining the incident as a non-emergency

positive correlation a relationship between two variables in which one increases as the other increases

positive reinforcement anything that strengthens behaviour because it is rewarding to the learner

prejudice an extreme attitude for or against a group, or a member of a group, based on characteristics that are assumed to be common to all members of the group

primacy effect the first information received has more influence than subsequent information

primary reinforcement anything that satisfies basic instincts

pro-social behaviour   behaviour that helps others

psychoanalytic theory   theory based on the idea that behaviour is caused by unconscious forces (Freud)

punishment   anything that weakens behaviour; makes a behaviour less likely to happen

random sampling   selecting participants on the basis that all members of the target population have an equal chance of being selected

recency effect   later information has more influence than earlier information

reinforcement   anything that strengthens behaviour; makes a response more likely to happen

repeated measures   an experimental design in which the same participants are in each condition

response   the activity that results from a stimulus

sampling   the method by which participants are selected for research

scapegoating   the process of blaming someone else for your problems

schema   a mental framework comprising what we already know, which we use to understand new experiences and to generate expectations of what is likely to happen

social categorisation   classifying people as members of either the in-group or the out-group

social desirability   the wish to be seen by others in a positive way

social facilitation   the change in performance that occurs when performing a task in the presence of others

social identity   the sense of who we are that is gained from membership of a group

social learning   human learning that takes place by observing others; observational learning

social loafing   putting less effort into a task that is being performed with others

social norms   the behaviours and beliefs that an individual is expected to show because of their social role or membership of a group

standardise   to make consistent so that results are comparable

standardised instructions   the identical instructions given to each participant in a study

stereotype   a rigid, generalised and simplified set of ideas about the characteristics of all members of a group

stereotyping   categorising someone as a member of a particular group and assuming they have the characteristics that all members of that group are thought to have

stimulus   anything (such as an event, object or person) that results in a change in someone's behaviour

stratified sampling   selecting participants so that they represent, proportionately, the target population

superego   the part of personality related to morals, to what we know is wrong, and to the kind of person we want to be (Freud)

survey   a way of gathering information by asking many people to answer standardised questions

systematic sampling   selecting participants at fixed intervals from the target population

unconditioned response   behaviour over which one has no control, which is automatic

unconditioned stimulus   anything that causes an unconditioned response

variable   anything that varies

vicarious reinforcement   when a person is reinforced by observing someone else; advertisers may use vicarious reinforcement by showing a model's positive experience of their product

INDEX